125

Film AND Fork

Volume 1

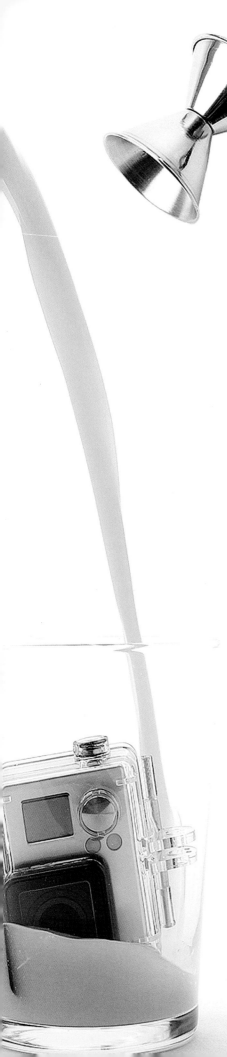

Editor-in-Chief
Max Abecassis

Chef/Writer/Recipes
Juan J. Janzen

Photography/Layout & Design
William Davis Moore

Concepts/Writer/Recipes
Merilyn Elizabeth McGonigal

Movie Consultant
Ryan M. Donahue

Edited by
Gregory J. Cafaro
Daniel Priest
Alison L. Carter

Website and Software Design
J. Allen Rager
Adam L. Minder
Alejandro P. Tapper
Ivars Blodnieks
Roy Skullestad

Special Contributions from:
Jacmel Ureña
Ted Smerken
Ben Jones
Thomas Pelkowski
Brielle Dunne
D.J. Valentine
J.M. Sanchez
Matthew J. Boor

Film and Fork © 2016 CustomPlay, LLC. All rights reserved.
Published by CustomPlay, LLC, Delray Beach, Florida.
www.customplay.com
Film and Fork is a Trademark of CustomPlay, LLC
Visit us at www.filmandfork.com

Printed in the United States of America
ISBN # 978-0-9972167-2-1
Library of Congress Control Number: 2016945439
First Edition

CustomPlay

CustomPlay's revolutionary Movie Companion App allows you to interact with your favorite movies like never before. Using your tablet, smartphone, laptop, or desktop you can instantly enjoy movie-related entertainment, information, and games. Our extensive features are available for a wide range of movies including everything from AFI classics to the latest blockbusters.

"I think this is the beginning of a beautiful friendship."
- Rick Blaine from Casablanca

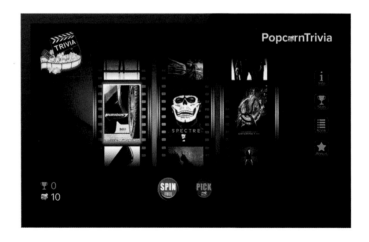

Test your overall cinema smarts across a variety of films with PopcornTrivia. Spin the wheels and select a film whose trivia you think you have the best chance of answering. Earning points and special film crew ranks along the way allows you to climb the leaderboard. PopcornTrivia puts a new spin on movie trivia.

"Shall we play a game?"
- Joshua from Wargames

About

At CustomPlay, we work with movies. What we mean is, we analyze every aspect of a movie. We try to figure out why the stormtroopers in *Star Wars: A New Hope* are all left-handed. We search Google Maps for the location of the house that Noah built for Allie in *The Notebook*. We even find you the exact tires used on the cars in *Mad Max: Fury Road*, if you were so inclined to purchase them for your own War Rig!

Like any job you do on an empty stomach, your mind begins to wander, and before you know it, you are thinking about food. We still can't watch that scene in *Inglourious Basterds* where Hans Landa orders the strudel ("Wait for the cream") without wanting one for ourselves. Instead of pushing those thoughts aside, we rolled with them. Often, it's easy to create a recipe for what the characters are eating on-screen, such as the sauce that Clemenza teaches Michael how to make in *The Godfather*. Sometimes it's tricky. *Predator*, for instance, a movie about a group of soldiers being hunted by a killer alien, doesn't readily supply too many culinary inspirations. It wasn't until the 50th time that we heard the iconic line "Get to the choppa!" as "Get to the 'lamb-choppa'!" Then, voilà! A delicious lamb chop dinner with a blood orange salad was created. It's truly an amazing feeling when you create an entertaining recipe experience that captures the essence of an iconic movie moment that had nothing to do with food.

This book is dedicated to the courage of the aspiring
actors and actresses who, while waiting tables, dream
of their big break.
Salud!

Menu

Alice in Wonderland (2010)
Mad Hatter's Mad Tea: lavender tea with honey-lavender syrup, vodka, and lavender bitters..........**160**

Aliens (1986)
Facehugger Crab: fried soft-shell crabs with arepas, orange-papaya purée, and grapefruit salsa..........**86**

Anchorman (2004)
Scotchy Scotch Scotch: blended Scotch, single malt Scotch, honey syrup, and fresh ginger..........**138**

Ant-Man (2015)
It's All About the Rosé: charcuterie with grilled pork loin, bacon-wrapped dates, and grilled peach crostini..........**184**

Crazy Stupid Fine Waffles: banana-apricot waffles with ricotta-mascarpone mousse and amaretto-apricot syrup..........**188**

Back to the Future (1985)
Enchantment Under the Seafood Medley: angel hair pasta with creamy white wine sauce, jumbo shrimp, and scallops..........**76**

Doc's Plutonium Cake: lemon cakes with raspberry and lemon buttercream filling, served with lemon curd..........**80**

The Big Lebowski (1998)
The Dude's White Russian: vodka, Kahlúa, and half and half..........**124**

Walter's Bowling Ball Burger: beef burger with potato latke bun and savory apple sauce..........**126**

The Breakfast Club (1985)
The Breakfast Cocktail: vodka, cream liqueur, apricot brandy, and Fruit Loops-infused milk..........**84**

Butch Cassidy & the Sundance Kid (1969)
Etta's Braised Beef: braised beef with bacon, carrots, and potatoes..........**44**

Bolivian Buñuelos: fried dough with guava syrup and served with candied plantains..........**48**

The Cabin in the Woods (2012)
The Merman: silver tequila, pineapple juice, and Blue Curaçao..........**162**

A Christmas Story (1983)
Flick's Hot Toddy: bourbon, apple brandy, and warm apple cider..........**74**

Citizen Kane (1941)
The Newspaper Baron: Lobster Newburg with caviar and brioche croutons..........**16**

Rosebud: apple tarts with strawberry glaze..........**20**

Deadpool (2016)
Pooljob Chimichanga: Kahlúa and Baileys Irish Cream, served with chorizo chimichangas..........**246**

Fifty Shades of Grey (2015)
The Contract: bourbon, sweet vermouth, bitters, and muddled cherries..........**192**

Bondage Bird: chicken breast stuffed with Italian sausage, spinach, and cheese, served with red wine cherry sauce and figs..........**194**

Fight Club (1999)
Big Moosie's Chicken Breasts: spicy chicken breasts served with quinoa, black beans, and banana-mango salsa..........**130**

Paper Street Cake Co.: pink champagne cake with buttercream frosting..........**134**

Forrest Gump (1994)
The Fruit of the Sea: coconut shrimp and lemon shrimp served with lemon and pineapple sauces..........**110**

A Box of Chocolates: chocolate truffles coated in cocoa powder, nuts, and coconut..........**114**

The Godfather (1972)
The Corleone Family Sunday Sauce: classic pasta with meatballs, sausages, and fresh basil..........**52**

Clemenza's Cannoli: cannoli with sweet ricotta filling and chocolate chips..........**56**

Goodfellas (1990)
Cutty and Water: Cutty Sark whisky and water..........**102**

Halloween (1978)
The Boogeyman: bourbon, orange juice, pumpkin ale, pumpkin purée, and autumn spices..........**70**

The Hangover (2009)
Hair of the Tiger: Bloody Mary with rye vodka, carrot juice, orange juice, pickle brine, spices..........**150**

Harry Potter & the Prisoner of Azkaban (2004)
Moonlight Lemonade: fresh lemonade with vodka, lavender bitters, lavender sugar, and peppermint..........**140**

The Hateful Eight (2015)
Blood and Snow: rye whiskey, blood orange juice, and cherry liqueur, served with blood orange syrup..........**198**

Bloody Tart: mocha tart with Oreo crust and blood orange syrup..........**200**

Home Alone (1990)
The Wet Bandit: eggnog with cognac, dark rum, milk, cream, and winter spices..........**100**

How to Train Your Dragon (2010)
Berk's Beer Float: stout beer ice cream float with beer-infused chocolate syrup..........**152**

Inception (2010)
The Kick: shot of vodka and cinnamon liqueur dropped into an energy drink..........**154**

Inception Turducken: pork sausage stuffed inside a duck, inside a chicken, inside a turkey, served with hasselback potatoes and tarragon-cherry sauce..........**156**

Inglourious Basterds (2009)
Aldo's Smoky Mountain Scalps: beef brisket served with German potato salad..........**142**

Landa's Apple Strudel with Cream: strudel with cinnamon, nutmeg, rum, almond, and apple filling..........**146**

Jaws (1975)
The Shark Attack: schnapps, vodka, and grenadine..........**60**

Amity Island Clam Chowder: New England clam chowder with seasoned Oyster crackers..........**62**

Life of Pi (2012)
Vishnu's Delight: grilled mahi-mahi served with conch salad and Mousseline sauce..........**164**

Pi's Pie: mango pie with blueberry sauce..........**168**

Mad Max: Fury Road (2015)
Not Your Mother's Milk: bourbon, simple syrup, vanilla, and whole milk..........**204**

Mad Max's Meat Pie: sirloin steak, prosciutto, celery, carrots, and savory herbs..........**206**

The Martian (2015)
Space Spuds: roasted potatoes, mashed potatoes, and purple skillet potatoes, served with Italian sausage..........**210**

Mark's Mashed Potato Truffles: chocolate-potato truffles coated in powdered fruit, cocoa powder, and ground pistachios..........**214**

Mission: Impossible - Rogue Nation (2015)
Turandot Dumplings: duck and shiitake mushroom dumplings served with curry, cilantro, and kimchi sauces..........**218**

Moroccan Cheesecake: goat cheese cheesecakes served with honey-lemon vinaigrette..........**222**

Predator (1987)
Get to the Lamb Choppas: lamb chops with spicy adobo, served with blood orange salad..........**92**

Dutch Chocolate Muddy Mousse Cake: chocolate cake with a chocolate mousse center..........**96**

The Princess Bride (1987)
Battle of Wits: red wine with blackberry liqueur, lemon juice, and cola..........**90**

Psycho (1960)
The Bloody Marion: Bloody Mary with vodka, tomato juice, horseradish, and Worcestershire sauce..........**38**

Kandy Korn Cake: vanilla cake with white, orange, and yellow buttercream frosting..........**40**

The Revenant (2015)
Revenge: icy granita made with blackberries, raspberries, chokecherry jelly, and huckleberry syrup..........**226**

Rocky (1976)
Southpaw Ribs: beef ribs with bourbon-cherry barbeque sauce, served with sweet potato wedges..........**66**

The Shining (1980)
REDRUM: white rum, moonshine, blood orange juice, and cherry juice..........**72**

The Silence of the Lambs (1991)
Buffalo Bill's Liquid Lotion: rum, banana liqueur, pineapple juice, and coconut milk..........**104**

The Census Taker: shallot tart topped with chicken liver, served with fava beans and red wine sauce..........**106**

Singin' in the Rain (1952)
Chestnut Cheddar Chive Chicken: chestnut crusted chicken tenderloins, served with chickpea salad..........**24**

Right in the Kisser Cake: deconstructed cake with strawberry frosting and glazed berries..........**28**

SPECTRE (2015)
Polpo di SPECTRE: grilled octopus with red pepper sauce and chorizo sausage..........**230**

The Cuckoo Nest: chocolate cake and fried dough nest with white cake eggs..........**234**

Star Wars: The Force Awakens (2015)
General Hux's Chicken: breaded chicken with ponzu sauce and brown rice..........**238**

Jakku Muffins: matcha pistachio muffins topped with honey..........**242**

Ted (2012)
Pot Brownies: flower pot-shaped chocolate brownies topped with mint ice cream..........**172**

Titanic (1997)
The Velvety Rose: champagne and stout beer..........**118**

Sweet Pea Lamb: lamb loin with mint sauce, served with sweet peas and fava beans..........**120**

Vertigo (1958)
The Green Judy: absinthe, crème de menthe green, crème de cacao, and melon liqueur..........**32**

Spiral of Madness: lemon bundtlette cakes, honey-vanilla glaze with candied lemons..........**34**

The Wizard of Oz (1939)
The Tin Man's Heart Beet: roasted beet and arugula salad, served with caramelized scallops..........**8**

Dorothy's Ruby Red Cake: red velvet cake with cream cheese icing, served with lemon curd..........**12**

The Wolf of Wall Street (2013)
Azoff's Fish Bowl: vodka, rum, Blue Curaçao, pineapple juice, and lemon-lime soda punch..........**178**

8-Balls and Lemons: mini lemon donuts coated in powdered sugar..........**180**

Wreck-It Ralph (2012)
Sugar Rush Milkshake: vanilla cotton candy milkshake with vodka, served in a candy-coated glass..........**176**

The Tin Man's Heart Beet

*"A heart is not judged by how much you love,
but by how much you are loved by others."
– The Wizard of Oz from The Wizard of Oz*

The Tin Man's Heart Beet is comprised of layers of roasted heart-shaped beets. The naturally sweet veggies contain powerful nutrients that help protect against heart disease and lower blood pressure. The heart-shaped beets are surrounded by a healthy serving of scrumptiously tender caramelized scallops, fresh arugula, and orange slices. This dish is sure to keep your body well oiled and your heart beeting!

The Tin Man's Heart Beet

Hands-On: 30 min
To Plate: 1 hr 30 min
Serves: 4

Ingredients:

Roasted Beets:
3 large red beets
2 large yellow beets
2 tbsp olive oil
1/4 cup sherry vinegar
1/2 cup water
1/2 cup arugula, for garnish
1 orange, segments only, for
  garnish

Beet Purée:
1/2 cup leftover beets
2 tsp Dijon mustard
2 tsp honey
1/8 cup sherry vinegar
3/4 cup canola oil
Salt and pepper, to taste

Scallops:
1 tbsp olive oil
1 lb bay scallops
Salt and pepper, to taste
1/4 cup white wine

Directions:

Roasted Beets:
Preheat oven to 400 degrees.

Rinse the beets, trim off the greens, and coat beets with olive oil.

In a casserole dish, add the beets, vinegar, and water, then cover with foil. Roast until fork-tender, about 1 hour.

Allow to cool.

Peel the beets and slice them into even 1/4-inch slices. Stack five slices, alternating colors, and cut the stack with a heart-shaped cookie cutter. Set aside. Use the leftover beet pieces for creating the beet purée.

Beet Purée:
In a blender, add the leftover beet pieces, mustard, honey, and vinegar, then blend. Slowly incorporate the oil. Season with salt and pepper.

Scallops:
In a large nonstick skillet over medium-high heat, heat olive oil.

Pat the scallops dry with paper towels, then sprinkle each side with salt and pepper. Add the scallops to the skillet, and cook until the underside is caramelized, about 2 minutes. Flip the scallops, add white wine, and caramelize the second side, about 1 minute.

Serve scallops with a heart-shaped stack of beets and garnish with arugula, beet purée, and orange segments.

Not only did the makeup and costumes in *The Wizard of Oz* cause the actors discomfort, they also caused a few serious health scares. Actor Buddy Ebsen was originally cast as the Tin Man, but he had a severe allergic reaction to the aluminum dust in his makeup and spent two weeks in the hospital. When Jack Haley took over, the makeup was changed to aluminum paste, which got into one of his eyes and gave him an eye infection that kept him out of work for a week. To top it all off, his costume weighed 40 pounds and did not allow him to sit down at all.

Dorothy's Ruby Red Cake

"It's always best to start at the beginning,
and all you do is follow the Yellow Brick Road."
– Glinda from The Wizard of Oz

You don't have to travel over the rainbow to enjoy this delightful dessert! Dorothy's Ruby Red Cake has two layers of red velvet cake coated with blue cream cheese icing. The scrumptious slice of cake is served atop a yellow brick road created with a sweet lemon curd. Now, take three bites and think to yourself, "There's no taste like homemade treats!"

Dorothy's Ruby Red Cake

Hands-On: 45 min
To Plate: 4 hrs 10 min
Serves: 4

Ingredients:

Lemon Curd:
3 eggs
1 cup white sugar
1/3 cup lemon juice
4 tbsp unsalted butter
2 tsp lemon zest

Dorothy's Ruby Red Cake:
3 medium beets
2 1/2 cups cake flour
1 tsp salt
2 tsp baking powder
1 cup milk
1/2 cup orange juice
3 tbsp white wine vinegar
16 tbsp unsalted butter
2 1/2 cups sugar
1 tbsp vanilla extract
4 eggs
1/4 cup Wilton red fondant

Cream Cheese Icing:
4 oz cream cheese, softened
4 tbsp unsalted butter, softened
1 tsp vanilla extract
1 cup powdered sugar
Blue food coloring

Directions:

Lemon Curd:
In a double boiler over simmering water, whisk eggs, sugar, and lemon juice continuously until ribbons form, about 7 minutes.

Fold in butter, zest, and strain through a mesh sieve to get rid of lumps. Cover and allow to thicken in the refrigerator, about 4 hours.

Dorothy's Ruby Red Cake:
Preheat oven to 400 degrees.

Wrap the beets in aluminum foil and roast until fork-tender, about 50 minutes. Remove from oven and allow them to cool.

In a blender, purée the beets.

Set the oven to 350 degrees.

In a bowl, whisk together the flour, salt, and baking powder.

In another bowl, combine 1 cup of the beet purée, milk, orange juice, and vinegar.

In a stand mixer, add the butter, sugar, and vanilla. Take turns adding an egg, 1/3 of the flour mixture, and 1/3 of the beet mixture until all the ingredients are fully incorporated.

Grease two 9-inch cake pans. Pour mixture into the pans and bake until the cake is done, about 30 minutes. Allow the cakes to cool completely before removing them from the pans.

Cream Cheese Icing:
In a medium bowl, blend together the cream cheese, butter, vanilla, and sugar. When the mixture is smooth, begin adding the food coloring until the desired color is achieved.

Apply a thin coat of the frosting to the cakes and allow it to harden in the refrigerator for 1 hour. Once the crumb coat has set, finish frosting the cakes.

Garnish with a thin bow made of the red fondant and create a yellow brick road with the lemon curd.

The iconic Ruby Red Slippers worn by Judy Garland in *The Wizard of Oz* are considered among the most famous and valuable costume pieces in cinema history. A number of pairs were made for the film, but only five are known to have survived to this day. In August of 2005, a crafty thief stole the pair on display at the Judy Garland Museum in Grand Rapids, Minnesota, and disappeared into the mist. The shoes have yet to be recovered. Not to worry though, one of the pairs can be seen on display at the Smithsonian Institution.

THE NEWSPAPER BARON

"I warn you, Jedediah, you're not going to like it in Chicago. The wind comes howling in off the lake and gosh only knows if they ever heard of Lobster Newburg."
- Charles Foster Kane from Citizen Kane

This Lobster Newburg recipe features a decadent combination of fresh lobster, caviar, brandy, creamy butter, and brioche croutons. Brioche is a bread of French origin that adds elegance to any meal with its golden color and melt-in-your-mouth texture. With every bite of this flavorful dish, you'll be feeling as rich as the Newspaper Baron himself.

THE NEWSPAPER BARON

Hands-On: 1 hr
To Plate: 3 hrs
Serves: 4

Ingredients:

2 fresh lobster tails
3 tbsp unsalted butter, divided
1/2 cup carrot, diced
1/2 cup onion, diced
1/2 cup celery, diced
2 tbsp tomato paste
1/4 cup brandy
3 cups heavy cream
Coarse salt, to taste
Freshly ground white pepper, to
    taste
2 shallots, peeled and minced
Cayenne pepper, to taste
Freshly ground nutmeg, to taste
1 tbsp brandy
1 large egg yolk, at room
    temperature
1 tbsp fresh-squeezed lemon
    juice
1 oz American sturgeon caviar
Brioche croutons

Directions:

Preheat oven to 350 degrees.

In a large bowl, prepare an ice water bath big enough to hold the lobster tails.

In a steamer basket over boiling water, cover and steam the lobster tails for 4 minutes. As soon as you remove them from the steamer, immerse the tails in the ice water bath to stop the cooking, about 5 minutes.

Crack the tails open and carefully remove the meat, keeping it in pieces as large as possible. Reserve the meat and the shells separately.

In a roasting pan, place the lobster shells and roast for 12 minutes, turning occasionally every 4 minutes, or until nicely colored and fragrant. Remove from the oven and set aside.

In a large saucepan over medium heat, heat 2 tablespoons of butter. Add the carrot, onion, and celery, and sauté for about 4 minutes, or just until the vegetables begin to soften. Add the tomato paste and sauté for another minute, until well incorporated. Stir in the reserved lobster shells, followed by 1/4 cup of the brandy. Cook for about 3 minutes, stirring to deglaze the pan. Add the cream, stir to blend, and raise the heat. Bring to a simmer. Season with salt and pepper and cook gently, stirring occasionally, for about 1 hour, or until very thick and well seasoned.

Remove the sauce from the heat and pour it through a fine-mesh sieve into a clean container, pressing on the solids to extract all of the flavors. Discard the solids and set the sauce aside.

In a medium sauté pan over medium-low heat, heat the remaining tablespoon of butter. Add the shallots and season with cayenne and nutmeg. Cook, stirring constantly, for about 2 minutes, or until the seasonings are fragrant.

Add the reserved lobster meat and sauté for 1 minute. Add the remaining tablespoon of brandy, stirring to deglaze the pan. Add the reserved cream sauce, raise the heat, and bring to a simmer.

Remove from heat, and, using a slotted spoon, transfer an equal portion of the lobster meat to each plate.

In a small bowl, place the egg yolk. Whisk a bit of the lobster cream sauce into the egg yolk to temper it, and then whisk the egg mixture into the sauce.

Pour the sauce over the lobster on each plate and add the lemon juice. Add an equal portion of caviar to each plate, and garnish with Brioche croutons. Season with salt and pepper to taste. Serve immediately.

In the film, Charles Kane's influence is best portrayed by his manipulation of American public opinion in favor of the Spanish-American War. To achieve this, he used an unethical practice called "yellow journalism", which presents little or no legitimately researched news. This type of journalism uses eye-catching headlines and sensationalism to sell more newspapers. Kane filled his newspaper, *The Inquirer*, with criticism of Spain's administration of Cuba, and anti-Spanish propaganda. His goal, however, wasn't to help the United States or Cuba, it was to increase *The Inquirer*'s circulation.

ROSEBUD

"I'll tell you about Rosebud. How much is it worth to you?"
- Raymond from Citizen Kane

These apple tart roses are inspired by the most beautiful and everlasting symbol in Charles Foster Kane's life: the decorative emblem on his childhood sled. Thin apple slices are used to create the sweet, delicate petals of the rosebud, which sit inside a delicious doughy crust. The strawberry preserve topping creates a lovely rose-colored glaze for this elegant dessert.

ROSEBUD

Hands-On: 1 hr 35 min
To Plate: 3 hrs
Serves: 4

Ingredients:

Dough:
1 1/4 cups all-purpose flour
1 tbsp sugar
1/4 tsp salt
8 tbsp unsalted butter, very cold, and cut into 1/2" cubes
3 tbsp ice cold water

Filling:
2 Honeycrisp apples
3 tbsp lemon juice
4 tbsp unsalted butter, divided
1/2 cup brown sugar, divided
1/4 cup strawberry preserves

Directions:

Dough:
In a medium-sized mixing bowl, combine flour, sugar, and salt. Work the butter into the flour, until the mixture looks like a coarse meal. Add in ice water and combine. The mixture should come together like a ball. Add more ice water if it's too dry. Form the dough into a disk, cover tightly with plastic wrap, and chill, about 1 hour.

On a well-floured surface, roll out the dough to 1/4-inch thickness. Use a cup about 4 inches in diameter to cut out rounds of dough.

In a buttered muffin tin, fit a round into each of the cups, pushing the dough up the sides. When the muffin tin is complete, place it in the freezer.

Rosebud Filling:
Remove cores from apples. Using a mandolin or a very sharp knife, cut the apples into very thin, half-moon-shaped slices.

In a bowl, toss the apples with the lemon juice to keep them from turning brown.

Preheat oven to 375 degrees.

Melt 2 tablespoons of butter and combine with 1/4 cup of brown sugar. Pour mixture over the apples and combine.

Microwave apples until soft and pliable enough to roll, about 1 minute.

Melt the remaining 2 tablespoons of butter and combine with remaining 1/4 cup of brown sugar. Brush the bottom of each dough cup with the mixture.

Remove muffin tins from freezer. To form the roses, place about 7 slices of apples on a flat surface, laying them out horizontally. Place each slice so it overlaps the previous slice by half. Tightly roll the apples from one end to the other, and place it in the muffin tin. Add more apple slices to fill in each tart.

Bake for 25 to 30 minutes until crust is golden and apples are cooked through.

Glaze the roses by warming the strawberry preserves and brushing over each apple rose.

At the end of *Citizen Kane*, Raymond the butler claims to have heard Charles Foster Kane whisper "Rosebud". However, Kane is alone in his room when he dies. When Orson Welles was asked about this by his friends, he paused and responded, "Don't you ever tell anyone of this." One fan theory is that the opening scene takes place from Raymond's point-of-view.

CHESTNUT CHEDDAR CHIVE CHICKEN

*"Chester chooses chestnuts, cheddar cheese with chewy chives.
He chews them, and he chooses them. He chooses them, and
he chews them. Those chestnuts, cheddar cheese, and chives in
cheery, charming chunks."*
- Diction Coach from Singin' in the Rain

Getting ready for the talking pictures doesn't have to be a chore. Chin up, channel your inner chef, and choose to cook this chestnut crusted chicken, with cheddar cheese, chewy chopped chives, and chickpea salad on the side. What's better than chicken, cheese, and chives? It's a charming meal for your children, or even your best chum! Choose this chestnut cheddar chive chicken and, while everyone chews, they'll chuckle and cheer!

CHESTNUT CHEDDAR CHIVE CHICKEN

Hands-On: 45 min
To Plate: 45 min
Serves: 4

Ingredients:

Chestnut Cheddar Chive Chicken:

8 chicken tenderloins
Kosher salt, to taste
Freshly ground black pepper, to
  taste
1/2 cup chestnut flour
2 tbsp canola oil
1 cup leek, finely chopped
2 garlic cloves, finely minced
1/2 tsp dry thyme
1/4 cup dry white wine
1 1/2 cups chicken broth
1 cup milk
1 cup sharp cheddar cheese,
  shredded
1/2 cup fresh chives, chopped,
  plus more for garnish
Edible flowers, for garnish

Chickpea Salad:

15 oz chickpeas, drained and
  rinsed
2 tbsp fresh basil, chopped
2 tbsp fresh Italian parsley,
  chopped
2 tbsp fresh lemon juice
4 tsp extra-virgin olive oil
1 small garlic clove, pressed
1/3 cup freshly grated Parmesan
  cheese
Kosher salt, to taste
Freshly ground black pepper, to
  taste

Directions:

Chestnut Cheddar Chive Chicken:

Season chicken with salt and pepper to taste.

In a shallow dish, add flour, and then dredge the chicken tenderloins until coated. Shake off excess and set aside.

In a large skillet over medium-high heat, heat the oil. When the oil is shimmering, add chicken and cook until browned on both sides, about 4 minutes per side. Remove chicken and set aside. Add leek, garlic, and thyme, then cook for 3 minutes. Add wine, and continue cooking while scraping up any browned bits until the wine has almost evaporated, about 2 minutes. Stir in broth and milk, then bring to a simmer while stirring often, and cook until the sauce has thickened slightly, about 1 minute.

Return the chicken to the skillet and simmer until the chicken is cooked through, about 4 more minutes. Remove chicken from skillet and set aside.

Remove skillet from heat, and then stir cheddar and chives into the sauce until the cheese is melted.

To serve, spoon the sauce over the chicken, and garnish with extra chopped chives, edible flowers, and the chickpea salad.

Chickpea Salad:

In a medium bowl, combine chickpeas, basil, parsley, lemon juice, extra-virgin olive oil, and garlic. Add Parmesan cheese and toss gently. Season salad with kosher salt and freshly ground black pepper to taste.

A popular myth is that milk or ink was added to the water to make the raindrops in the legendary "Singin' in the Rain" number visible on camera, but Gene Kelly and his co-director, Stanley Donen, have debunked this by explaining that it was actually achieved through the simple use of backlighting.

RIGHT IN THE KISSER CAKE

"Here's one thing I've learned from the movies!"
- Kathy from Singin' in the Rain

Leading lady Lina Lamont may be a star of silent films, but in synchronized sound she's a teensy bit too much. If movies have taught us anything, it's that the best way to shut someone's pie hole is to throw a cake at it. Cake? This isn't a cake. It's "a shimmering, glowing star" in the dessert firmament. Glamorously glazed berries, whipped cream, pink strawberry frosting, and pieces of crumbly cake are staged in an elegantly deconstructed fashion. This sweet treat is fit for any Hollywood diva, even if it's right in the kisser.

RIGHT IN THE KISSER CAKE

Hands-On: 20 min
To Plate: 55 min
Serves: 4

Ingredients:

Right in the Kisser Cake:

1 box Pillsbury Classic White
   Cake Mix
1/3 cup oil
3 eggs
Cooking spray
Whipped cream, for serving
Strawberry frosting, for serving
Granola, for garnish

Glamorous Glazed Berries:

3/4 cup granulated sugar
2 tbsp cornstarch
1 cup cold water
3 oz package strawberry flavored
   gelatin
16 oz fresh strawberries
6 oz fresh raspberries

Directions:

Right in the Kisser Cake:

Preheat oven to 350 degrees.

In a large bowl, add cake mix, oil, and eggs. Mix until well combined.

Grease a 13 x 9-inch cake pan, pour in the mixture, and then bake until a toothpick inserted into the cake comes out clean, about 35 minutes. Allow the cake to cool completely before removing it from the pan.

Crumble several pieces of cake onto the plate, and serve with a dollop of whipped cream, a dollop of strawberry frosting, and a few glazed berries. Garnish with granola and fresh strawberries.

Glamorous Glazed Berries:

In a saucepan over medium heat, cook the sugar, cornstarch, and water until thickened, stirring constantly. Stir in the strawberry gelatin, and then whisk constantly until smooth.

Reserve 8 of the nicest strawberries for garnish. Slice the rest of the strawberries, place them in the warm gelatin mixture, then add the raspberries to the mixture.

In *Singin' in the Rain*, it appears that Kathy Selden (Debbie Reynolds) is doing some voice dubbing for Lina Lamont (Jean Hagen), but it's not Debbie Reynolds' voice that we hear singing the song. It's actually the voice of actress Betty Noyes, who also provides the voice for the somber ballad "Would You".

THE GREEN JUDY

*"Scottie, do you believe that someone out of the past,
someone dead, can enter and take possession of a living being?"
- Gavin Elster from Vertigo*

Being pulled into the darkness? Here, drink this straight down. It's just like medicine. The Green Judy is concocted with a mystical combination of fresh lemon juice, crème de menthe, crème de cocoa, triple sec, melon liqueur, and is enlivened with a hint of absinthe. Known as "The Green Fairy", absinthe is a potent spirit with a beautifully complex herbal flavor and a mysterious reputation. This ethereal cocktail will have you dreaming in green.

Serves: 1

Ingredients:

Splash of absinthe
1 oz crème de cacao
3 oz crème de menthe green
1 oz triple sec
3 oz Midori
2 tbsp simple syrup
2 tbsp fresh lemon juice
Fresh mint, for garnish
Lime twist, for garnish

Directions:

Add a splash of absinthe to a reservoir glass. Gently swirl the glass around so that the absinthe coats the inside. Discard the excess.

In a cocktail shaker with ice, add the crème de cocoa, crème de menthe, triple sec, Midori, simple syrup, and lemon juice. Shake vigorously until chilled, and then strain into the reservoir glass.

Garnish with fresh mint and a lime twist.

SPIRAL OF MADNESS

"Somewhere in here I was born, and there I died.
It was only a moment for you. You took no notice."
– Madeleine Elster from Vertigo

Deep in the Muir Woods, surrounded by towering redwood trees, it's easy to lose one's mind. Do you believe a dessert recipe from the past, something delicious, can enter and take possession of your kitchen? Somewhere in here we baked them, and there we ate them. You'll certainly take notice of these insanely moist and thrillingly delicious bundtlette cakes that are drizzled with a sweet honey-vanilla glaze. Served with candied lemon peels, you'll become obsessed with these luscious little lemon spirals.

SPIRAL OF MADNESS

Hands-On: 45 min
To Plate: 1 hr 15 min
Serves: 4

Ingredients:

Glaze:
1/2 tsp pure vanilla extract
1/2 cup water
1 cup sugar
1/4 cup honey
2 tbsp unsalted butter

Spiral Bundtlette Cakes:
Cooking spray
Zest of 2 lemons
1 cup sugar
13 tbsp unsalted butter, at room
   temperature
1 tsp fresh lemon juice
1/2 tsp vanilla extract
3 eggs, lightly beaten
1 1/2 cups all-purpose flour
1/2 tsp baking powder
1/4 tsp kosher salt

Candied Lemon Spirals:
2 lemons
1 cup sugar
1 cup water

Directions:

Glaze:
In a small saucepan, add vanilla extract, water, sugar, honey, and butter. Heat the mixture over low heat, just until the sugar dissolves. Increase heat to medium and cook for 5 minutes. Remove from heat and let cool for 10 minutes.

Spiral Bundtlette Cakes:
Preheat oven to 325 degrees.

Generously spray a bundtlette pan with cooking spray, then dust with flour, tapping out any excess.

In a small bowl, combine the lemon zest and sugar.

In the bowl of an electric mixer, beat the butter on medium speed until smooth, about 2 minutes. Add the lemon sugar mixture, lemon juice, and vanilla extract, then beat until fluffy, about 5 minutes. Add the eggs, one at a time, beating well before each new addition.

In a large mixing bowl, sift together flour, baking powder, and salt.

Reduce the mixer's speed to low, and then add the flour mixture in three separate batches.

In a pastry bag, add the batter and pipe into the prepared bundtlette pan, filling each cup about 3/4 full. Bake until a toothpick inserted into the middle of a cake comes out clean, about 15 minutes. Allow bundtlettes to cool slightly before removing from pan.

Carefully dip each bundtlette in the glaze, allowing them to absorb the mixture. Place the bundtlettes on a wire rack to allow excess glaze to drip off. Garnish with a lemon spiral prior to serving.

Candied Lemon Spirals:
Using a citrus peeler, peel four long strips from the lemons.

In a small saucepan, boil the lemon peels in water for 30 seconds, remove completely from water, then repeat. Drain water and set peels aside.

In a saucepan over medium heat, add water and sugar. Stir the mixture until a thick syrup is created, about 6 to 8 minutes. Add the lemon peels and cook in the syrup for 15 minutes.

Using culinary tweezers, remove the peels from the syrup and carefully wrap them around the tweezers to form a spiral shape. When dried, the lemon peels will keep their spiral shape.

The Muir Woods in *Vertigo* is actually the Big Basin Redwoods State Park, home to the oldest Ancient Coast Redwoods south of San Francisco. Established in 1902, it is California's oldest state park, offering over 80 miles of trails which traverse the park's 2,000-foot change in elevation. The park is great for leisurely drives, hiking, and camping.

THE BLOODY MARION

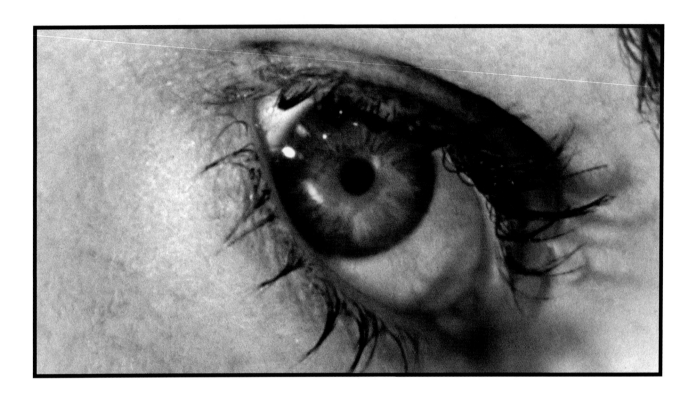

"Ahhh!"
- Marion Crane from Psycho

What better way to welcome guests than with a Bloody Marion! It's much safer than taking a shower. This bloodcurdlingly refreshing cocktail is inspired by one of the most famous scenes in movie history! While this may be Marion's last shower, this grisly cocktail is loaded with antioxidants that will give you a nice boost along with the added health benefits. Finish off the cocktail with a piece of watermelon carved into a crane. And be sure to share some with Mother.

Serves: 1

Ingredients:

The Bloody Marion:

1 lemon wedge
1 lime wedge
2 oz premium vodka
4 oz tomato juice
2 dashes Cholula hot sauce
2 tsp prepared horseradish
2 dashes Worcestershire sauce
1 pinch ground black pepper
1 pinch smoked paprika

Crane Garnish:

1 watermelon
1 celery stalk
1 mint sprig

Directions:

The Bloody Marion:

Fill a highball glass with ice and set aside.

Squeeze the lemon and lime wedges into a cocktail shaker, then drop them in. Add the remaining ingredients and fill with ice. Shake gently and strain into the prepared glass.

Garnish drink with watermelon crane, a celery stalk, and a nice sprig of mint.

Crane Garnish:

Cut off a round disk of the watermelon's rind, creating a nice-sized canvas to work with. Draw a simple bird pattern on the skin and, using a sharp paring knife, carefully cut out the desired shape.

KANDY KORN CAKE

*"We do have a vacancy, twelve in fact.
Twelve cabins, twelve vacancies. Candy?"
- Norman Bates from Psycho*

Norman is certifiably mental about his Kandy Korn, so what better way to honor their tricolored goodness than an insanely large wedge of Kandy Korn cake! Go cuckoo as you plunge your knife deep into the heart of this moist and dense dessert. Ree! Ree! Ree! Stab your fork into a slice, and go totally mental as you murder every last crumb. We all go a little mad sometimes. Haven't you?

KANDY KORN CAKE

Hands-On: 1 hr 30 min
To Plate: 2 hrs 30 min
Serves: 4

Ingredients:

Cake:
22 tbsp unsalted butter
2 1/3 cups sugar
1 1/4 tsp salt
5 eggs
4 tsp vanilla extract
2 tsp baking powder
2 2/3 cups flour
1 1/3 cups milk
White food coloring
Orange food coloring
Yellow food coloring

Buttercream Frosting:
8 tbsp unsalted butter
4 cups powdered sugar
3 tbsp heavy cream
1/2 cup shortening
1 tsp vanilla extract
White food coloring
Orange food coloring
Yellow food coloring

Directions:

Cake:
Preheat oven to 325 degrees.

In a mixer, beat butter until smooth. Add sugar and salt, then mix until fluffy, about 3 minutes. Add the eggs one at a time and incorporate completely. Add in vanilla and baking powder. Set mixer to low and add flour in three separate additions alternating with the milk, until well blended.

Separate the batter equally into three bowls and tint one white, one orange, and one yellow with food coloring.

Spray two muffin pans with cooking spray. Evenly distribute the different colored batter in the muffin pans.

Bake until each cake is fully cooked and a toothpick comes out clean, about 20 minutes.

Place the cakes in the refrigerator to cool.

Buttercream Frosting:
In a mixer, beat butter until smooth, then add powdered sugar, heavy cream, shortening, and vanilla extract. Mix until blended.

Separate the frosting into three bowls and tint one white, one orange, and one yellow with food coloring.

Stack a white cake on top of an orange cake and then stack those on top of a yellow cake.

Using a bread knife, shave a cone shape out of the three stacked cakes.

Glue the layers together by placing orange and yellow frosting between the cake layers. Add a white crumb coat using the white frosting to create a smoother surface for which to pipe on the frosting. Place the cake in the refrigerator to set, about 30 minutes.

Pipe the outside of the cake with a star tip, using the white, orange, and then yellow frosting.

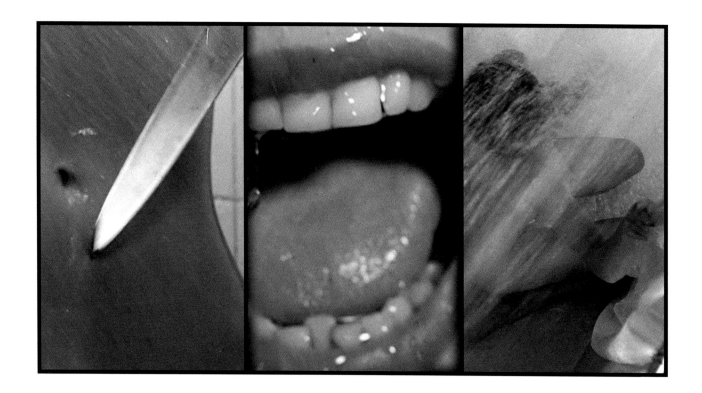

Janet Leigh and her body double, Marli Renfro, a nude model that appeared on the September 1960 cover of *Playboy*, both portrayed the character Marion Crane in *Psycho*'s infamous shower scene. Myra Jones, who was Marion's stand-in during the lighting set-ups, was tragically murdered in 1988 by an obsessed *Psycho* fan who mistook Jones for Renfro.

Etta's Braised Beef

"Do you know what I wish? That once, you'd get here on time!"
- Etta Place from Butch Cassidy and the Sundance Kid

This dish has plenty of fixin's to feed hungry outlaws on the dodge. The beef is slowly braised in a Dutch oven with bacon, red wine, brandy, aromatic herbs, spices, and pearl onions. In the Old West, a Dutch oven was the most revered piece of cooking equipment. It was brought to America in the early 18th century, and quickly grew in popularity across the states. Paul Revere is credited with refining the design of the pot, which has barely changed since the days of the Old West.

Etta's Braised Beef

Hands-On: 1 hr 15 min
To Plate: 2 hrs 40 min
Serves: 4

Ingredients:

Braised Beef:
2 fresh parsley sprigs
2 fresh rosemary sprigs
2 fresh thyme sprigs
2 fresh bay leaves
2 tbsp olive oil, divided
4 slices fatty bacon, halved
2 lbs boneless beef chuck, cut
  into 4" cubes
Kosher salt, to taste
Freshly ground black pepper, to
  taste
4 tbsp tomato paste
3 tbsp all-purpose flour
1/2 cup Cognac
1/2 bottle Burgundy wine
4 1/2 cups beef stock, divided
4 tbsp unsalted butter
1 tbsp sugar
2 tbsp whiskey
2 cups pearl onions, blanched
  and peeled
2 garlic cloves, finely minced
1 tsp nutmeg

Carrots:
1/2 lb baby carrots, peeled
1 tbsp unsalted butter
1 tbsp honey

Carrot Purée:
1 1/2 lbs carrots, peeled
2 garlic cloves
1/2 cup beef stock
1/4 tsp ginger, grated
1/4 cup heavy cream
Salt and pepper, to taste

Roasted Potatoes:
1 lb rainbow fingerling potatoes,
  halved
2 tbsp olive oil
1 tsp kosher salt
2 garlic cloves, crushed
2 tbsp fresh thyme leaves

Directions:

Braised Beef:
Using kitchen twine, tie up the parsley, rosemary, thyme, and bay leaves into a small bunch.

In a large Dutch oven over medium heat, drizzle 1 tablespoon of the olive oil. Cook the bacon strips until crisp. Remove bacon from the Dutch oven, and set aside on a paper towel-lined plate.

Season the beef with salt and pepper, then add it to the Dutch oven. Fry the beef in the bacon fat until evenly browned on all sides, about 10 minutes. Remove the beef and set aside. Add the tomato paste and flour, then stir to combine. Remove from heat, pour in the Cognac, and carefully ignite the liquid. When the flame dies down, place Dutch oven back on the heat. Stir in the wine, 4 cups of the beef stock, and the tied herbs, then return the beef to the pot. Stir until the liquid starts to thicken, about 15 minutes. Cover the pot, reduce heat to low, and simmer for 1 hour.

In a saucepan over medium heat, add butter, sugar, whiskey, and the remaining 1/2 cup of beef stock. Stir, add the pearl onions, and cook until tender.

In the Dutch oven, add the cooked pearl onions, garlic, and nutmeg, then simmer for another 45 minutes, stirring occasionally.

Carrots:
In a pot of boiling water, add carrots and cook until tender, about 3 to 4 minutes. Drain carrots and pat dry.

In a large skillet over medium-low heat, melt the butter. Add the carrots and honey, then cook until the carrots are slightly browned, about 8 minutes.

Carrot Purée:
Chop carrots into equal-size disks.

In a pot, add carrots, garlic, beef stock, and ginger. Bring to a boil, reduce heat to low, and cover. Simmer until the carrots are tender, about 25 minutes. Uncover pot and allow the mixture to cool for 10 minutes.

In a blender, carefully add the carrot mixture, cream, and purée until smooth.

Roasted Potatoes:
Preheat oven to 425 degrees.

In a large mixing bowl, add the potatoes, olive oil, salt, garlic cloves, and thyme. Toss well to combine.

On a baking sheet lined with aluminum foil, spread out the potatoes evenly and bake for 40 minutes. Flip the potatoes after 20 minutes.

The actual Etta Place is a bit of mystery. Her real name may have been Ethel Bishop, a music teacher who some think might have also been a prostitute. "Etta" is thought to have either been a typo by the Pinkerton Detectives on her wanted posters, or a mispronunciation by Spanish speakers who couldn't pronounce "Ethel" after she moved to South America. "Place" was the maiden name of Harry Longabaugh's (the Sundance Kid) mother. When Etta and Sundance were together, they introduced themselves as Mr. and Mrs. Harry Place.

Bolivian Buñuelos

"Well, you know it could be worse.
You get a lot more for your money in Bolivia, I checked on it."
- Butch Cassidy from Butch Cassidy and the Sundance Kid

Don't worry fellas, Bolivia is sweeter than it seems. These traditional treats, called buñuelos, are sweet, crispy fried fritters that are sprinkled with powdered sugar and orange zest. The buñuelos are served with candied plantains, an exotic guava syrup, and a cream cheese sauce. This is a dessert worth making, we checked on it.

Bolivian Buñuelos

Hands-On: 55 min
To Plate: 1 hr
Serves: 4

Ingredients:

Guava Syrup:
1 cup guava paste
2 tbsp water

Cream Cheese Sauce:
8 oz cream cheese
1/2 cup sugar
1 tbsp cornstarch
1/2 cup milk
1 tbsp margarine
1 tsp lemon juice
1 tsp vanilla extract

Plantains:
1 very ripe plantain, peeled and
    sliced
4 tbsp unsalted butter
1 tsp vanilla extract
1 tsp cinnamon
2 tbsp brown sugar

Buñuelos:
2 cups flour
2 cups milk
2 eggs
1 tsp baking powder
1/2 tsp sugar
1/2 tsp salt
3 cups cooking oil
2 cups granulated sugar
3 tbsp cinnamon
1 tbsp orange zest, for garnish

Directions:

Guava Syrup:
In a small saucepan, add the guava paste and water. Bring the mixture to a boil, while stirring constantly. Remove from heat, let cool, and pour into a squeeze bottle. Serve sauce at room temperature.

Cream Cheese Sauce:
In a saucepan over medium heat, add cream cheese, sugar, and cornstarch, then stir constantly until all the cheese has melted. While stirring constantly, add the milk, and then remove from heat. Add the margarine, lemon juice, and vanilla, then stir until well incorporated. Place mixture in a squeeze bottle and serve at room temperature.

Plantains:
In a large skillet over medium-low heat, melt butter. Add plantains and fry until golden brown. Remove from heat and sprinkle them with vanilla, cinnamon, and brown sugar.

Buñuelos:
In a large bowl, combine the flour, milk, eggs, baking powder, sugar, and salt.

In a medium saucepan, heat 3 cups of oil over medium heat to 350 degrees.

In a mixing bowl, combine the granulated sugar and cinnamon.

Heat a buñuelo mold in the hot oil for 1 minute before dipping it onto the surface of the batter, allowing batter to cling onto the mold. Dip the mold back into the hot oil, and hold it there until the buñuelo falls off the mold, shake gently if needed to loosen the batter. Continue frying the buñuelo until both sides are golden brown, about 1 minute per side. Remove cooked buñuelo from the oil and transfer to a cooling rack.

Sprinkle each buñuelo with powdered sugar and orange zest. Serve with plantains, guava syrup, and cream cheese sauce. Enjoy!

When the real Butch and Sundance left America, they went to Argentina first, not Bolivia. Once they arrived, they put their life of crime aside for four years and became peaceful ranchers. Butch and Sundance did not go to Bolivia until after Etta Place returned to America.

The Corleone Family
Sunday Sauce

"Come over here, kid, learn something.
You never know, you might have to cook for twenty guys someday."
- Clemenza from The Godfather

The best way to feed a hungry mob is to whip up the Corleone Family Sunday Sauce. Put on some Sicilian music and follow Clemenza's directions: start off with a little bit of oil, and then you fry some garlic, and throw in the tomatoes. The tender Sicilian-style meatballs are made with a trio of ground meats and browned to perfection before being shoved into the sauce along with the Italian sausage. Add a little bit of wine, toss in a little bit of sugar, and that's the trick.

The Corleone Family Sunday Sauce

Hands-On: 1 hr 15 min
To Plate: 2 hrs
Serves: 4

Ingredients:

The Corleone Family Sunday Sauce:

2 tbsp olive oil
3 cloves garlic, chopped
2 (28 oz) cans of tomatoes, chopped
2 (6 oz) cans tomato paste
4 Italian sausages, grilled and sliced
1/4 cup Francis Ford Coppola Director's Cut Dry Creek Valley Zinfandel, or a dry red wine
1/4 cup sugar

Meatballs:

1/3 lb ground veal
1/3 lb ground pork
1/3 lb ground beef
1 slice white sandwich bread, torn
3/4 cup milk
1 egg
2/3 cup freshly grated Parmesan cheese
1/3 cup grated pecorino
2 tbsp fresh flat-leaf parsley, chopped
2 tsp kosher salt
1/4 tsp freshly ground pepper
1 small clove garlic, minced
1/2 cup all-purpose flour
2 tbsp olive oil

Pasta:

1 lb spaghetti pasta

Directions:

The Corleone Family Sunday Sauce:

In a large pot over medium heat, heat the oil. Add the garlic and cook, stirring for a few minutes, being careful not to burn the garlic. Add the tomatoes, tomato paste, and cook, stirring continuously, for 5 minutes to combine until a relatively smooth consistency is reached. Add the sausage and meatballs, stir to coat the meat. Add a little bit of wine, and a little bit of sugar. Reduce the heat to medium-low and simmer for at least 20 minutes, stirring occasionally to prevent scorching.

Meatballs:

In a large mixing bowl, combine the meats, bread, milk, egg, cheese, parsley, salt, pepper, and garlic. Using your hands, fold all the ingredients together until well mixed. Be careful to not overmix, otherwise the meat will become dense and heavy.

In a large bowl, add the flour. Form golf ball-size servings by scooping out 1/8-cup portions of meat and gently rolling them between your hands. Toss meatballs into the flour as you work.

In a large skillet over medium heat, heat the olive oil. Add the meatballs and cook until golden brown, about 8 to 10 minutes. The internal temperature should be about 155 degrees.

Pasta:

Bring a large pot of lightly-salted water to a boil. Add pasta and cook for 8 to 10 minutes or until al dente. Drain and serve with The Corleone Family Sunday Sauce.

Legendary film director Francis Ford Coppola originally thought *The Godfather* was going to be a flop. His reasoning for putting in a sauce recipe is because he felt that if the film was going to tank, at the very least the audience would learn how to make some good Italian food.

Clemenza's Cannoli

"Leave the gun. Take the cannoli."
– Clemenza from The Godfather

When leaving a crime scene, always remember to leave the gun and take the cannoli. Truly the epitome of Sicilian pastries, these irresistible treats have a sweet, creamy filling made with fresh ricotta cheese, powdered sugar, and a hint of vanilla. The crispy shells are created with the addition of Marsala wine to the cannoli dough, which is then fried to perfection before being stuffed. Prior to serving, the ends are carefully dipped in chocolate chips. Have some fun. Make the cannoli!

Clemenza's Cannoli

Hands-On: 1 hr 30 min
To Plate: 2 hrs
Serves: 4

Ingredients:

Shells:
2 cups all-purpose flour
2 tbsp unsalted butter
1 tsp sugar
Pinch of salt
3/4 cup Marsala wine
1 egg white, beaten
Vegetable oil, for frying
Powdered sugar, for dusting

Ricotta Filling:
3 cups fresh ricotta cheese
1/2 cup powdered sugar
1/2 tsp vanilla

Garnish:
1 cup mini-semisweet chocolate
   chips

Directions:

Shells:
In a large bowl, mix together the flour, butter, sugar, and salt. Add only enough wine to form a fairly firm dough. Knead dough for a few minutes, until smooth, then form into a ball, wrap in plastic wrap, and let sit at room temperature for one hour. Cut the dough in half, and roll to a 1/4-inch thickness. Cut dough into 5-inch squares. Place a stainless steel tube diagonally across each square and wrap the dough around the tube. Seal the edges with a little beaten egg white.

In a large pan, heat the oil until it reaches a temperature of 375 degrees.

Place tubes into the oil and cook until golden, about 4 minutes. Carefully, remove from the oil, tubes will be hot! Cool and gently slide the cannoli shell from the tube.

Ricotta Filling:
Strain the fresh ricotta at room temperature for 30 minutes to remove the excess water.

In a bowl, mix the strained ricotta with the powdered sugar and vanilla. Chill in the refrigerator for at least 30 minutes.

After the filling has been chilled, fill in each cannoli shell.

Garnish:
In a microwave safe bowl, heat 3/4 cup semi-sweet chocolate at 50% power for 30 seconds, stir, and repeat until melted. Place mixture into a squeeze bottle to garnish the plate. Use the remaining 1/4 cup of chocolate chips to garnish the cannoli. Drizzle the melted chocolate onto the plate and dust with powdered sugar.

The line "Leave the gun" was scripted, but "Take the cannoli" was ad libbed by actor Richard S. Castellano, who plays Pete Clemenza. This bit of improvisation helped turn a mundane piece of dialogue into one of the most famous film quotes of all time.

THE SHARK ATTACK

"This shark, swallow you whole.
Shakin', tenderizin'. Down you go."
- Quint from Jaws

This is the perfect drink to enjoy while lounging on the beach during the Fourth of July. The refreshing island punch is made with blue Pucker, orange vodka, and lemon-lime soda. Add a couple splashes of grenadine to create the effect of blood in the water and watch your guests' jaws drop. "Here's to swimmin' with bowlegged women!"

Serves: 1

Ingredients:

2 oz Island Punch Pucker
2 oz orange vodka
6 oz lemon-lime soda
A few drops grenadine, for effect

Directions:

In a cocktail shaker with ice,
combine the Island Punch Pucker
and vodka. Shake vigorously until
chilled, and then strain into a glass.

Top with lemon-lime soda, and drop
a small amount of grenadine in the
center of the glass to create the blood
effect.

AMITY ISLAND
CLAM CHOWDER

"Amity, as you know, means 'friendship'."
- Mayor Vaughn from Jaws

You yell, "Soup!" and everybody says, "Huh? What?" You yell, "Clam chowder!" and everyone comes running with a spoon in their hands. Rich and creamy, this traditional New England clam chowder is made with shucked fresh clams, hearty cream, and just the right amount of potatoes. You're gonna need a bigger bowl.

AMITY ISLAND CLAM CHOWDER

Hands-On: 40 min
To Plate: 1 hr
Serves: 4

Ingredients:

Chowder:

1 cup water
1/2 tsp salt
10 oz fresh Manila clams
2 tbsp unsalted butter
1 medium onion, finely diced
2 celery stalks, quartered
   lengthwise, then sliced into
   1/4" pieces
3 tbsp all-purpose flour
1 1/4 cups vegetable stock
1 cup heavy cream
2 bay leaves
2 medium Idaho potatoes, cut
   into 1/2" cubes

Crackers:

1 cup oyster crackers
1 tsp olive oil
1 tbsp Old Bay seasoning

Directions:

Chowder:

In a large pot, bring 1 cup of water to a boil. Add 1/2 teaspoon of salt and the clams. Steep fresh clams until shells open.

Remove clams from the water, place in a bowl, and let cool. Reserve the water in the pot for the base of the stock. Once the clams are cool to the touch, set aside 8 clams in their shells for garnish, and shuck the rest from their shells.

In large pot over medium-high heat, melt 2 tablespoons of butter. Add the onion and celery, and sauté until softened, stirring frequently. Stir in the flour, a little at a time, then add the water left from the steeped clams, vegetable stock, cream, bay leaves, and potatoes. Bring to a simmer, stirring constantly, until the mixture thickens, about 20 minutes.

While the chowder is simmering, preheat oven to 350 degrees.

In a medium bowl, toss the crackers, olive oil, and seasoning together. Spread the seasoned crackers on a baking sheet, and bake for 6 minutes.

When the potatoes in the chowder are tender, add the clams to the chowder long enough to warm the clams.

Top each serving with two of the reserved clams, and garnish with oyster crackers.

Jaws was filmed in Martha's Vineyard, Massachusetts. Director Steven Spielberg chose to use Martha's Vineyard as the fictional town of Amity for two reasons: the town had never been used as a location in a film prior to *Jaws*, and the ocean was very shallow. At 12 miles offshore the water was only about 30 feet deep, which allowed for easy maneuvering of the mechanical shark.

SOUTHPAW RIBS

"You're breaking the ribs."
- Paulie from Rocky

If you want to go the distance, go for the ribs. These big, beefy ribs are generously slathered with a spicy dry rub and then slowly roasted in the oven until they're knockout tender. Before serving, the ribs are brushed with a bourbon-cherry barbeque sauce that's sure to get your taste buds blissfully punch-drunk. The Southpaw Ribs are served with grilled sweet potato wedges and a tangy cherry salsa.

SOUTHPAW RIBS

Hands-On: 45 min
To Plate: 10 hrs 25 min
Serves: 4

Ingredients:

Rocky's Ribs:
8 beef back ribs
2 bay leaves

Dry Rub:
1/4 cup brown sugar
2 tbsp paprika
2 tsp chili powder
2 tsp garlic powder
2 tsp onion powder
1 tsp ground black pepper
1 tsp Kosher salt
1/2 tsp cayenne pepper

Balboa's Bourbon-Cherry Barbecue Sauce:
2 tbsp unsalted butter
1 medium yellow onion, chopped
2 medium cloves garlic, minced
2 cups tomato sauce
1 1/2 cups fresh pitted cherries
1/4 cup dark brown sugar
1/4 cup fresh-squeezed orange juice
1/4 cup molasses
1/4 cup cider vinegar
1/2 cup bourbon
1/2 tsp ancho chili powder
1/2 tsp dry mustard
1 tsp kosher salt
1 tsp freshly ground pepper
1/2 tsp cayenne pepper

Baked Sweet Potatoes:
3 medium sweet potatoes, cut into wedges
1 1/2 tbsp olive oil
1/2 tsp ground chipotle powder
Pinch of chili flakes
Salt, to taste
Pepper, to taste

Cherry Salsa:
1 cup sweet black cherries, pitted
3 green onions, thinly sliced
1 inch of ginger, grated
Zest and juice of 1 lime
Pepper, to taste

Directions:

Rocky's Ribs:
In a small bowl, add all the dry rub ingredients and mix well to combine.

Pat the ribs dry and dust them liberally with the dry rub.

Place a bay leaf on top of each of the ribs and tightly seal them in aluminum foil. Allow the ribs to marinate in the refrigerator for 2 hours prior to cooking.

Preheat oven to 200 degrees.

On a baking sheet, place the ribs in a single layer, covered with foil, and bake them in the oven until desired tenderness, about 8 hours for a fall-off-the-bone tenderness. Allow them to rest 20 minutes prior to serving.

Serve ribs with sweet potatoes, cherry salsa, and a nice coat of the cherry barbecue sauce.

Balboa's Bourbon-Cherry Barbecue Sauce:
In a saucepan over medium heat, melt butter, add onion, and cook until softened, about 5 minutes. Add garlic and cook until fragrant, about 30 seconds. Stir in remaining ingredients and bring to a boil. Reduce heat and simmer until slightly thickened, about 30 minutes.

In a blender, carefully purée the hot mixture. Strain and pour into a squeeze bottle.

Baked Sweet Potatoes:
Preheat oven to 400 degrees.

In a large bowl, coat the sweet potato wedges with olive oil and spices.

On a baking sheet, bake the sweet potatoes, skin side down, until fork-tender, about 30 minutes.

Cherry Salsa:
Chop the pitted cherries and place them in a medium-sized bowl. Add the sliced green onions, ginger, lime zest, lime juice, and black pepper. Stir to combine before serving.

Rocky was one of the first films to feature the Steadicam. It was used to film Rocky's run through Philadelphia, Adrian and Rocky's date at the ice skating rink, and Rocky's fight with Apollo Creed. The innovative device was developed by Garrett Brown, who also operated the Steadicam on such films as *The Shining*, *Indiana Jones and the Temple of Doom*, *Casino*, and many more. Its very first use was in 1976's *Bound for Glory*, which won an Oscar for Best Cinematography.

Halloween

"You know, it's Halloween.
I guess everyone's entitled one good scare."
—Sheriff Leigh Brackett from Halloween

The Boogeyman is lurking just around the corner. Before he gets you, trick-or-treat yourself to this spiced pumpkin drink. It's to die for! Full of fall flavors, this creepy cocktail is perfect for celebrating Halloween on any spooky night. He's gonna get you, he's gonna get you, he's gonna get you, he's gonna get you!

Serves: 1

Ingredients:

1 1/2 oz Maker's Mark
  bourbon
1 oz orange juice
1 tbsp pumpkin purée
1 tbsp maple syrup
A pinch of cinnamon
A pinch of nutmeg
A pinch of pumpkin spice
2 dashes orange bitters
3 oz Fat Head's Imperial
  Pumpkin Ale, chilled
Orange peel, for garnish

Directions:

In a cocktail shaker with ice, add
the bourbon, orange juice, pumpkin
purée, syrup, cinnamon, nutmeg,
pumpkin spice, and bitters.

Shake vigorously until chilled and
strain into a glass.

Top with chilled pumpkin beer and
garnish with an orange peel carved
like a jack-o-lantern.

REDЯUM

"Redrum. Redrum. Redrum."
- Danny Torrance from The Shining

All work and no play making you a dull boy? Head to the Gold Room and ask Lloyd to craft you a drink that truly shines. After all, some drinks are like people: some 'shine' and some don't. The Redrum is mixed with a bloody good combination of blood orange juice, cherry juice, maraschino liqueur, rum, and a little shine…moonshine, that is. You'll want to enjoy this murderously delightful cocktail forever, and ever, and ever… Cheeers, Johnny!

Serves: 1

Ingredients:

1 oz white rum
1/2 oz moonshine
2 oz blood orange juice
1 oz tart cherry juice
1/2 oz maraschino liqueur
1/2 oz simple syrup
Squeeze of fresh lime juice
Fresh raspberries, for garnish

Directions:

In a cocktail shaker with ice, add
rum, moonshine, blood orange juice,
cherry juice, maraschino liqueur, and
simple syrup, then shake vigorously
until chilled.

Strain into a champagne coupe.

Top with a squeeze of lime juice and
garnish with fresh raspberries.

Flick's Hot Toddy

"I triple-dog-dare you!"
Schwartz from A Christmas Story

It isn't Christmas without a little cinnamon. We triple-dog-dare you to try this delightfully warm holiday drink. Perfect for days when you've been stuck out in the cold or when you're trapped indoors with the extended family. The combination of bourbon, apple brandy, and Campari will warm you up while the sweet maple syrup soothes your throat. Leave out the liquor and you still have a deliciously warm treat for the little ones.

Serves: 1

Ingredients:

1 tbsp maple syrup
1 oz Wild Turkey bourbon
1 oz apple brandy
1/2 oz Campari
Apple cider, heated
3 whole cloves
3 whole allspice berries
Apple wedges, for garnish
Cinnamon sticks, for garnish

Directions:

In an 8 oz Irish coffee mug, add boiling water. Allow the water to heat the mug, then discard the water.

Add maple syrup to the bottom of the mug, followed by the bourbon, brandy, Campari, and cider.

Stir well and garnish with the cloves, berries, apple wedges, and cinnamon sticks.

ENCHANTMENT UNDER THE SEAFOOD MEDLEY

"Look! There's a rhythmic ceremonial ritual coming up!"
– Doc Brown from Back to the Future

When your existence depends on making two people fall in love, prepare them a meal that's truly extraordinary. This enchanting seafood medley is brimming with scallops and jumbo shrimp. The angel hair pasta is bathed in a flavorful cream sauce made with white wine, Parmesan cheese, and fresh herbs. With a wave of flavors, this deep-sea delight is apt to please anyone's aquatic palate. Be there or be square!

ENCHANTMENT UNDER THE SEAFOOD MEDLEY

Hands-On: 40 min
To Plate: 55 min
Serves: 4

Ingredients:

Dancing Shrimp:
4 jumbo shrimp, cleaned
1 tbsp olive oil
2 tbsp unsalted butter
2 garlic cloves, finely minced
1 tbsp lemon juice
Salt, to taste
Pepper, to taste

Under the Sea Pasta:
7 tbsp unsalted butter, divided
1 tbsp all-purpose flour
1 cup seafood stock
1 cup heavy cream
1/2 cup white wine
3 tbsp tomato purée
1/2 tsp saffron threads
1 lb scallops
Kosher salt, to taste
Freshly ground black pepper, to
    taste
1 cup Panko bread crumbs
1/3 cup freshly grated Parmesan
    cheese
2 tbsp fresh flat-leaf parsley,
    minced
1 tbsp fresh tarragon leaves,
    minced
1 tbsp minced garlic
16 oz angel hair pasta
Fresh sprigs thyme
Fresh sprigs rosemary
Cherry tomatoes, sliced

Directions:

Dancing Shrimp:
In a skillet over medium-high heat, heat oil. Add shrimp and sauté until pink. Add butter, garlic, lemon juice, salt, and pepper, stir, and then toss the shrimp in the mixture as it finishes cooking. Remove from heat and set aside.

Under the Sea Pasta:
In a medium saucepan over high heat, melt 4 tablespoons of the butter, and then add flour to make a roux, stirring continuously until a caramel color is achieved.

Add the stock, cream, wine, tomato purée, and saffron. Bring to a boil, lower the heat to medium, add the scallops, cook 3 minutes, and set aside. Continue cooking the sauce until reduced by half, about 10 minutes. Season with salt and pepper to taste.

In a saucepan, melt the remaining 3 tablespoons of butter. Add the Panko, Parmesan cheese, parsley, tarragon, and garlic, then cook until lightly toasted, about 5 minutes.

Cook pasta according to package instructions and toss it with the sauce before serving. Sprinkle pasta with the Panko mixture, and garnish with fresh thyme and rosemary. Serve with scallops and shrimp, then garnish with slices of cherry tomatoes and more Panko bread crumbs.

In *Back to the Future*, Marty's rendition of Chuck Berry's 1958 rock and roll classic "Johnny B. Goode" pays homage to a few other guitar legends aside from Berry. He finger taps like Eddie Van Halen, plays the guitar behind his head like Jimi Hendrix, flails around on his back like AC/DC's Angus Young, and kicks the amp like The Who's Pete Townshend.

DOC'S PLUTONIUM CAKE

"Doc, you don't just walk into a store and buy plutonium!"
– Marty McFly from Back to the Future

Great Scott! These little radioactive lemon treats will make your taste buds glow with delight. Much like Doc's plutonium-powered DeLorean, the cakes are fueled with a nuclear combination of fresh strawberries and lemon buttercream, and they are served over a tart lemon curd. With each bite, this dessert generates 1.21 "jigowatts" of flavor! The way we see it, if you're going to bake a cake, why not do it with some style?

DOC'S PLUTONIUM CAKE

Hands-On: 1 hr
To Plate: 4 hrs 30 min
Serves: 4

Ingredients:

Radioactive Lemon Cake:

16 tbsp unsalted butter, softened
2 cups granulated sugar
4 large eggs
2 large egg yolks
1 tsp salt
3 tsp baking powder
3 cups all-purpose flour
2 cups buttermilk
2 1/2 tsp vanilla extract
4 raspberries, thinly sliced

Strawberry Filling:

2 cups granulated sugar
2 cups fresh strawberries

Lemon Buttercream Filling:

8 tbsp unsalted butter, softened
3 cups powdered sugar
2 tbsp lemon juice
1 tsp lemon zest
1 tbsp heavy cream
Yellow food coloring

Lemon Curd:

5 egg yolks
1 cup sugar
1/3 cup lemon juice
Zest of 4 lemons
8 tbsp unsalted butter, cubed and chilled

Flux Capacitor Raspberry Sauce:

1/4 cup fresh raspberries
2 tsp granulated sugar
3/4 tsp cornstarch

Directions:

Radioactive Lemon Cake:

Preheat oven to 350 degrees.

In a bowl, mix the butter and sugar. Incorporate the 4 eggs into the mixture, one at a time, and then incorporate the 2 egg yolks.

In a large mixing bowl, whisk together the salt, baking powder, and flour. Add half of the dry mixture into the butter mixture and combine. Add 1 cup of the buttermilk and the remainder of the dry mixture, and then mix. Add the rest of the buttermilk and combine. Stir in the vanilla.

Grease a 9-inch baking pan and pour in the mixture. Bake until a toothpick inserted into the cake comes out clean, about 25 minutes. Remove from oven and allow to cool.

Strawberry Filling:

In a saucepan, bring the strawberries and sugar to a boil. Reduce heat and simmer for 40 minutes. Allow the mixture to cool completely before using.

Lemon Buttercream Filling:

In an electric mixer, beat butter for 1 to 2 minutes until fluffy. Slowly add powdered sugar, 1/2 cup at a time, until mixture is smooth. Add lemon juice and zest, then mix until combined. Add cream and mix at medium-high speed until light and fluffy, about 2 minutes. While mixing, add yellow food coloring to achieve the desired yellow color.

Lemon Curd:

In a metal bowl, whisk the egg yolks and sugar until smooth. Add lemon juice and zest, then whisk until smooth. In a double boiler, whisk the mixture until thickened, about 8 minutes.

Remove from heat, then stir in butter, one cube at a time. Strain through a mesh sieve to get rid of lumps. Cover and allow to thicken in the refrigerator, about 4 hours.

Flux Capacitor Raspberry Sauce:

In a small saucepan, combine the raspberries, sugar, and cornstarch, then bring to a boil. Reduce heat, then simmer for 5 minutes. Take off heat and let cool. The sauce will begin to thicken.

In a blender, purée the sauce. Strain it to remove the seeds, and then pour the smooth mixture into a squeeze bottle.

Assembly:

To serve, cut out disks of the Radioactive Lemon Cake using a 2-inch ring mold. Carefully slice off the tops and place some of the strawberry filling and lemon buttercream inside each mini cake. Top each mini cake with a dollop of the lemon buttercream filling and thinly sliced raspberries.

Slowly pour the lemon curd onto the plate until the bottom is covered. Gently place the mini cakes on top of the lemon curd and create the flux capacitor out of the raspberry sauce.

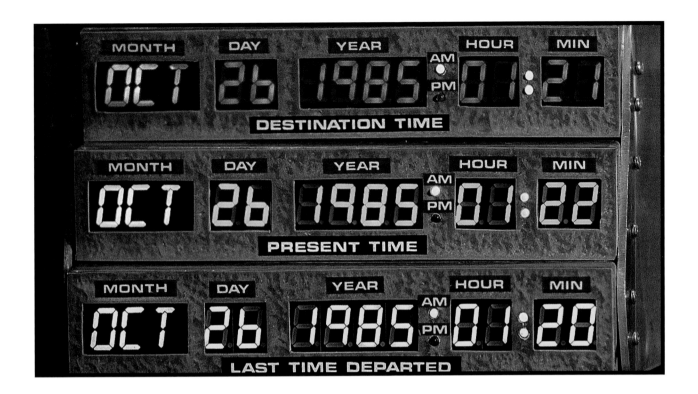

In *Back to the Future*, the readout colors on the DeLorean's time circuits are an homage to the red, yellow, and green lights on the machine built by Rod Taylor's character in the 1960 film *The Time Machine*.

the Breakfast Cocktail

"We're all pretty bizarre.
Some of us are just better at hiding it, that's all."
—Andrew Clark from The Breakfast Club

Dear Readers, we spent a whole Saturday pondering what our favorite drink is. At first, we thought maybe it was one of the stereotypical cocktail clichés. You know, a Jägerbomb, a Screwdriver, a Cosmo, or maybe even a Whiskey Sour. But what we found out is that each of us wanted something a little different. This breakfast-worthy cocktail incorporates cereal-infused milk, cream liqueur, apricot brandy, and vodka. How much vodka? Tons. Sincerely, The Beverage Club.

Serves: 1

Ingredients:

Cocktail:
5 oz Fruit Loops milk
1 oz vodka
1 oz RumChata
1/2 oz apricot brandy

Fruit Loops Milk:
1 cup Fruit Loops cereal
1 cup whole milk

Directions:

Cocktail:
In a cocktail shaker with ice, add Fruit Loops milk, vodka, RumChata, and brandy.

Shake vigorously until chilled and strain into a glass.

Fruit Loops Milk:
In a bowl, combine cereal and milk. Mix, cover, and refrigerate for 2 hours.

Strain the mixture and discard the solids.

FACEHUGGER CRAB

*"My mommy always said there were no monsters,
no real ones, but there are."*
- Newt from Aliens

No need to be afraid, they mostly come out at night. Mostly. The only thing you need to fear about this Facehugger Crab is the moment you take the last bite. The crispy, fried soft-shell crabs "hug" a helplessly delicious orange-papaya purée. Served with toasty arepas and a citrusy grapefruit salsa tail, this is a meal you won't want to detach from your face. One bite of this and it's game over, man. Game over!

FACEHUGGER CRAB

Hands-On: 1 hr 5 min
To Plate: 1 hr 10 min
Serves: 4

Ingredients:

Facehugger Crab:
1 cup milk
1 cup flour
8 soft-shell crabs, cleaned
Canola oil, for frying

Arepas:
2 cups Pan arepa flour
2 tsp kosher salt
2 1/2 cups warm water
2 tbsp vegetable oil

Grapefruit Salsa:
2 large red grapefruit, rinds removed and diced
1 large orange, rinds removed and diced
1 small papaya, diced
1 medium tomato, chopped fine
1 cup orange bell pepper, diced
1 cup red bell pepper, diced
1 jalapeño pepper, seeded and minced
1 small red onion, diced
2 tbsp fresh cilantro leaves, chopped
1 tbsp fresh ginger, grated
1 tbsp fresh orange juice
4 slices bacon, cooked and chopped
Salt, to taste

Orange-Papaya Purée:
1 large papaya, chopped
2 tbsp sugar
2 tbsp fresh orange juice

Directions:

Facehugger Crab:
In a mixing bowl, add the milk.

In another mixing bowl, add the flour.

In a deep stockpot, heat 3 inches of oil to 365 degrees.

Dip crabs in milk, then into the flour, making sure to coat them well. Fry them in the oil until crispy, about 3 minutes per side. Place fried crabs on a paper towel lined plate.

Serve crispy crabs with Orange-Papaya Purée, 2 arepas, and a nice tail of grapefruit salsa.

Arepas:
In a medium bowl, combine arepa flour and salt.

Make a well in the center of the bowl and add 2 1/2 cups warm water. Gradually incorporate dry ingredients, stirring until no dry lumps remain. Allow mixture to rest for 5 minutes.

Knead dough and divide into 1-inch balls then gently flatten to about 1/2-inch thick.

In a large nonstick skillet over medium heat, heat 1 tablespoon vegetable oil.

Add arepas, cover, and cook until golden brown, about 6 minutes. Uncover, flip, and continue cooking until other side is golden brown, about 6 more minutes. Allow to cool on a wire rack.

Grapefruit Salsa:
In a large mixing bowl, combine all ingredients.

Orange-Papaya Purée:
In a blender, add all ingredients and blend until smooth.

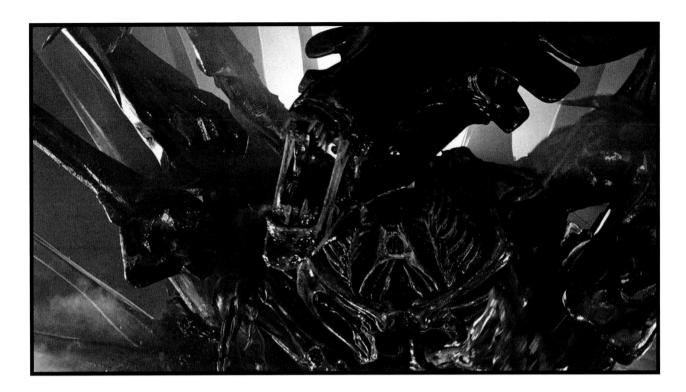

Aliens director James Cameron says of H.R. Giger's creature designs for the first film in the franchise, 1979's *Alien*, "All of Giger's designs have a real sexual undercurrent to them. And that's what I think horrified people about the Alien as much as anything is it worked on a kind of Freudian subconscious level…This film was never intended to be as much of a horror film as the first one. It was working on a different thematic level but I still wanted to be true to some of those ideas, some of those design concepts."

BATTLE OF WITS

"All right. Where is the poison? The battle of wits has begun.
It ends when you decide and we both drink,
and find out who is right... and who is dead."
–Man in Black from The Princess Bride

So, you've climbed the Cliffs of Insanity, defeated the Spanish swordsman, and taken down the giant. Next, you must challenge your enemy to a Battle of Wits! Mix together red wine, cola, blackberry liqueur, lemon juice, and orange bitters. Pour into two unmarked goblets, secretly add the iocane powder, then use your dizzying intellect while you enjoy this divine drink. Disclaimer: It's recommended that you spend a few years building an immunity to iocane before engaging in this Battle of Wits. Also, never get involved in a land war in Asia.

Serves: 1

Ingredients:

6 oz red wine
2 oz blackberry liqueur
2 oz fresh lemon juice
4 dashes orange bitters
4 oz cola, chilled

Directions:

In a cocktail shaker with ice, add the red wine, blackberry liqueur, lemon juice, and bitters.

Shake vigorously until chilled, then strain into two goblets.

Top with cola and serve.

GET TO THE LAMB CHOPPAS

"Get to the choppa!"
- Dutch from Predator

Get to the Lamb Choppa! Marinate it with Val Verde Adobo, a spicy sauce made from dried chiles, herbs, and vinegar! Come on! Eat it! Eat it! Come on! You'll want this recipe to stick around! Do it now!

GET TO THE LAMB CHOPPAS

Hands-On: 30 min
To Plate: 1 hr 30 min
Serves: 4

Ingredients:

Get to the Lamb Choppas:
4 bone-in lamb chops, frenched

Val Verde Adobo:
5 dried chipotle chiles
4 dried Ancho chiles
1 tsp cumin seeds
1 tsp coriander seeds
1/2 tsp ground allspice
1 1/4" piece cinnamon stick
1 tsp dried oregano
5 garlic cloves, roughly chopped
2 shallots, roughly chopped
2 tsp soft dark brown sugar
2 tbsp red wine vinegar
5 tbsp sherry vinegar
1 1/2 tsp salt, or to taste

Blood Orange Salad:
8 cherry tomatoes, halved
2 blood oranges, segments only
4 parsley sprigs, whole leaves
  only
4 cilantro sprigs, whole leaves
  only
2 tbsp dill, whole
1 tbsp whole, fresh oregano
  leaves
1 tsp extra-virgin olive oil

Directions:

Get to the Lamb Choppas:
Preheat oven to 450 degrees.

In a skillet over high heat, sear the lamb until the skin is golden brown, about 4 minutes per side. Let cool, rub on adobo, and cover the bones in foil.

On a baking tray, bake lamb until internal temperature reaches 125 degrees (for rare). Start checking at about the 10 minute mark. Let rest for 15 minutes. Carefully remove aluminum foil and slice the lamb.

Serve lamb with the blood orange salad and the Val Verde adobo.

Val Verde Adobo:
In a dry skillet over medium heat, toast the chiles just until they are warm and pliable. After they have cooled, discard the stems and the seeds from all the chipotles, and half the ancho chiles.

In a small saucepan, add the chiles and enough water to barely cover them. Bring to a boil, remove from the heat, and let soak for 30 minutes. Strain the chiles, making sure to reserve the liquid.

In a dry skillet over medium heat, toast the whole cumin and coriander seeds until fragrant, about 40 seconds.

In a food processor, purée the chiles, toasted seeds, allspice, cinnamon, oregano, garlic, shallots, sugar, and vinegar. Add just enough of the reserved chile soaking liquid to create the consistency of a paste. Season with salt to taste.

Blood Orange Salad:
In a bowl, lightly toss together all the salad ingredients.

In this scene from *Predator*, Dutch seems to survive a direct hit from the Predator's laser cannon with barely a scratch. However, watching it again in slow motion reveals that the blast hits Dutch's gun, which absorbs most of the impact.

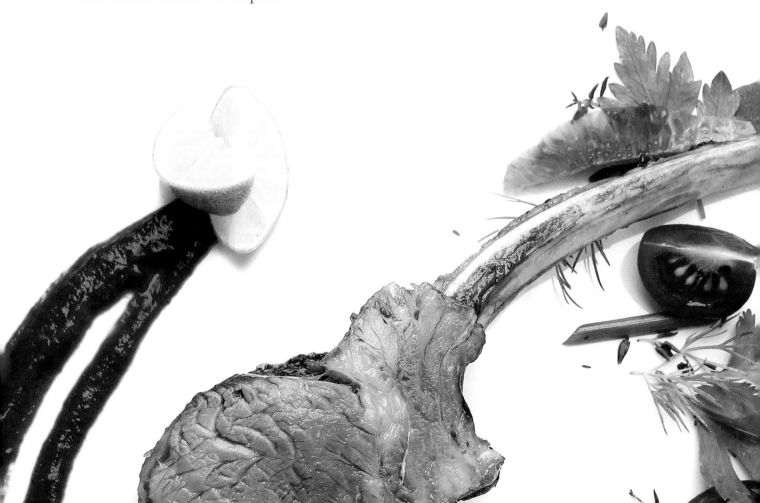

DUTCH CHOCOLATE MUDDY MOUSSE CAKE

"He couldn't see me."
- Dutch from Predator

Knock-knock! Hunting for a delicious dessert? The Dutch Chocolate Muddy Mousse Cake has a luscious chocolate mousse center sandwiched between two layers of delectable Dutch chocolate cake. The dessert is covered with a rich chocolate ganache icing and garnished with milk chocolate curls. This is the perfect treat to trick any would-be Predator. Catch it and kill it one slice at a time!

DUTCH CHOCOLATE MUDDY MOUSSE CAKE

Hands-On: 1 hr
To Plate: 3 hrs
Serves: 4

Ingredients:

Mousse:
1 2/3 cups heavy cream
4 large egg yolks, room temperature
1/4 cup sugar
2 tbsp light corn syrup
2 tbsp water
4 oz bittersweet chocolate, melted
1 tsp pure vanilla extract
Sea salt, to taste

Dutch Chocolate Cake:
Vegetable oil cooking spray
1/3 cup all-purpose flour
1/8 cup unsweetened Dutch-process cocoa powder
1/3 cup sugar
1/4 tsp baking soda
1/3 tsp baking powder
1/8 tsp salt
1 large egg, room temperature
1/8 cup whole milk
1 1/2 tbsp vegetable oil
1/4 tsp pure vanilla extract
1 milk chocolate bar, shaved into curls

Ganache:
1 cup heavy cream
8 oz semisweet chocolate chips
1 tbsp unsalted butter

Directions:

Mousse:
In an electric mixer fitted with a whisk attachment, add heavy cream and beat on medium-high speed until soft peaks form, about 3 minutes. Move to another bowl and refrigerate for 1 hour.

In the electric mixer fitted with a whisk attachment, add egg yolks and beat on high speed until pale and frothy, about 5 minutes.

In a small saucepan over high heat, bring sugar, corn syrup, and 2 tablespoons of water to a boil. Cook until large clear bubbles form, about 1 minute.

Reduce the mixer speed to medium-low and slowly pour the hot syrup into the bowl with the eggs. Raise speed to medium-high, and mix until slightly thickened, about 5 minutes. Stir in bittersweet chocolate, 1 teaspoon vanilla, and a pinch of salt.

In the bowl with the chilled whipped cream, fold in 1/3 of the chocolate mixture at a time. Pass the mixture through a large mesh sieve into a large bowl in order to remove any solids.

Dutch Chocolate Cake:
Preheat oven to 350 degrees.

Coat four 6-ounce ramekins with cooking spray.

In an electric mixer fitted with a paddle attachment, mix flour, cocoa powder, sugar, baking soda, baking powder, salt, egg, milk, oil, vanilla, and 1/8 cup water. Mix on medium-low speed until smooth, about 3 minutes.

In the coated ramekins, distribute the batter evenly, and bake until a toothpick inserted into the center comes out clean, about 20 minutes. Let cool completely before removing cakes from the ramekins.

Cut each cake in half, creating 8 disks of cake. Carefully spoon the mousse over 4 of the cakes. Cover each half of cake with its corresponding top. Refrigerate for 1 hour to set.

Ganache:
In a saucepan, add the heavy cream and bring it to a boil.

In a metal bowl, add the chocolate and pour in the heated cream. Let sit for 5 minutes without mixing. Then stir until smooth, add butter, and mix well.

Place the chilled cakes on a wire rack over a baking sheet, and pour on the ganache, evenly coating the 4 cakes.

Allow the chocolate to set before serving. Garnish with more ganache and the milk chocolate curls.

Before their final confrontation, the Predator misses seeing Dutch because his body heat is obscured by cold mud. In reality, the mud would warm up from Dutch's body heat in a matter of seconds, making him visible to the Predator's heat vision. This was confirmed by the Discovery Channel's *Mythbusters*. And just as icing on the cake, Dutch's eyes are not covered in mud, which should have made them visible to the Predator anyway.

THE WET BANDIT

"You guys give up? Or ya thirsty for more?"
- Kevin McCallister from Home Alone

When you get tired of Pepsi and want to switch to something a little more festive, give this lovely homemade eggnog a whirl. Made with whole milk, cream, vanilla, and a variety of winter spices, The Wet Bandit tastes like Christmas in a glass. For a nice buzz, spike the eggnog with a little cognac and spiced rum! Be sure to serve this holiday beverage with a "highly nutritious microwavable macaroni and cheese dinner" on the side. Merry Christmas, ya filthy animal!

Serves: 1

Ingredients:

1 large egg yolk
1 1/2 tbsp granulated sugar
3 oz whole milk
3 oz heavy cream
Pinch of salt
Pinch of nutmeg
Pinch of cinnamon
Pinch of ground allspice
Pinch of ground anise
1 tsp pure vanilla extract
1 oz cognac
1 oz dark rum
Whipped cream, for topping

Directions:

In a small saucepan over medium-high heat, combine the milk, cream, salt, nutmeg, cinnamon, allspice, and anise. Stir continually until mixture barely begins to simmer, then remove from heat.

In a small bowl, whisk the egg yolk and sugar until light and creamy.

Whisk a large spoonful of the hot milk mixture into the whisked egg mixture. Continue adding one large spoonful at a time in order to temper the eggs. Once all of the hot milk has been added to the eggs, pour the mixture back into the saucepan. Return to medium-high heat, whisking constantly, until mixture reaches 160 degrees. Remove from heat and stir in the vanilla, cognac, and rum.

Pour the eggnog into a glass container, cover with plastic wrap, and refrigerate until chilled. Top with whipped cream and sprinkle with cinnamon before serving.

Omit the alcohol for an enjoyable Christmassy eggnog.

Cutty & Water

"Hey, Spider! On your way over here,
bring me a Cutty and water, huh?"
- Tommy DeVito from Goodfellas

If you've always wanted to be a gangster, there's a couple of things you gotta learn. First and foremost, never rat on your friends. Next, if you're gonna hang around wiseguys, you gotta learn to drink like a wiseguy. Just remember to keep it simple and don't mess around with any of that fruity garbage. Stick to Cutty and water…no more, no less. And don't let them put you on a pay-no-mind list, kid. If it's not delivered promptly, shoot Spider in the foot.

Serves: 1

Ingredients:

2 oz Cutty Sark Scotch whisky
5 oz water

Directions:

In a Collins glass filled with ice, add the Scotch.

Fill the rest of the glass with water.

Stir to combine.

buffalo bill's
liquid lotion

"It rubs the lotion on its skin or else it gets the hose again."
- Jame "Buffalo Bill" Gumb from The Silence of the Lambs

Don't torture yourself over making a delicious cocktail. It's not that hard. It makes Buffalo Bill's Liquid Lotion with rum, banana liqueur, pineapple juice, and coconut milk, or else it gets the hose again. It shakes the lotion until chilled whenever it's told. Yes it will, Precious, won't it? Now, it drinks the liquid lotion, and when it's finished, it places the lotion in the basket.

Serves: 1

Ingredients:

2 oz light rum
2 oz organic full-fat
  coconut milk
1 oz pineapple juice
1/2 oz crème de bananas
1/2 oz simple syrup

Directions:

In a cocktail shaker with ice, add all ingredients.

Shake vigorously until chilled, and strain into a glass.

EST. 1991

BUFFALO BILL'S

LIQUID LOTION

It rubs the lotion on it's skin
or else it gets the hose again

the census taker

"A census taker once tried to test me. I ate his liver
with some fava beans and a nice Chianti."
– Hannibal Lecter from The Silence of the Lambs

Hannibal Lecter is a man with refined taste, especially when it comes to cuisine. These shallot tarte tatins are elegantly topped with seared liver. If you can't get your hands on a census taker, a chicken liver will do just fine. Be sure to serve the savory tarts with some fava beans and a nice Chianti reduction… Fft fft fft!

the census taker

Hands-On: 40 min
To Plate: 1 hr 40 min
Serves: 4

Ingredients:

Shallot Tarte Tatin:
20 shallots, peeled
2 cups of nice Chianti
2 bay leaves
2 sprigs fresh rosemary
2 sprigs fresh thyme
1 garlic clove, finely minced
1/4 cup honey
1 tbsp brown sugar
4 sheets puff pastry
Salt, to taste
Freshly ground black pepper, to
    taste

Chicken Liver:
1 tbsp vegetable oil, more if
    needed
4 chicken livers, cleaned
2 cloves garlic, finely minced
1/2 cup red wine vinegar
1 tbsp parsley
Salt, to taste
Freshly ground black pepper, to
    taste

Some Fava Beans:
1 cup fava beans, peeled
Salt, to taste
1/2 tbsp unsalted butter
1/2 tbsp olive oil

Directions:

Shallot Tarte Tatin:
In a pot of boiling salted water, blanch the shallots for 4 minutes, drain, let cool, and slice.

In a saucepan, place the sliced shallots, wine, bay leaves, rosemary, thyme, garlic, and honey. Bring to a boil, reduce heat, and simmer for 45 minutes. With a slotted spoon, remove shallots from the pan and set aside. Using a sieve, transfer the wine mixture into a clean saucepan. Add a tablespoon of brown sugar, bring to a boil, reduce heat to a simmer, and continue reducing sauce until a thick consistency is reached.

Preheat oven to 360 degrees.

In four 4-inch tart molds, distribute the shallots evenly and top with a sheet of puff pastry. Gently press the pastry down around the shallots.

Bake until the pastry is puffed and golden brown, about 10 minutes. Allow the tarts to cool then flip them over. Pour the red wine sauce over the tarts, reserving some of the sauce to garnish the plate.

Place a liver on top of each of the tarts, serve with some fava beans, and a bloody good helping of wine sauce.

Chicken Liver:
In a pan over medium-high heat, heat the oil. Sear the livers on both sides. Add garlic and red wine vinegar, then cook until the internal temperature of the liver reaches 165 degrees.

Some Fava Beans:
In a small pan over medium heat, add the butter and olive oil. When the butter has melted, add the beans and sauté for 2 minutes. Remove from heat and season with salt to taste.

Anthony Hopkins is responsible for the now-iconic slurping noise that Hannibal Lecter makes when he talks about the census taker. He made it up right on the spot, and it stuck. Lecter's nickname, Hannibal the Cannibal, is appropriate not just because he literally eats people; he is also able to "consume" people on a mental and emotional level by using his intelligence and psychiatric expertise to gain power over them.

The Fruit of the Sea

"There's pineapple shrimp, lemon shrimp,
coconut shrimp, pepper shrimp…"
– Bubba Blue from Forrest Gump

Enjoy some of the tastiest variations of the "fruit of the sea" with this shrimpspirational dish! Have a taste of lemon and herb marinated shrimp with a zesty sauce, and crispy coconut encrusted shrimp with a tangy dipping sauce consisting of pineapple, orange marmalade, fresh orange juice, and ginger. Your friends will go on and on about them.

The Fruit of the Sea

Hands-On: 1 hr 15 min
To Plate: 1 hr 15 min
Serves: 4

Ingredients:

Lemon Shrimp:
1 lb large shrimp, peeled and deveined
Zest of 1 lemon
Kosher salt, to taste
Freshly ground black pepper, to taste
2 tbsp fresh thyme, chopped
1 orange, cut into wedges, for garnish
Fresh cilantro sprigs, for garnish

Lemon Sauce:
1 medium yellow bell pepper, de-seeded and ribs removed
1/4 cup lemon juice
1/4 cup sugar
1/4 cup olive oil

Coconut Shrimp:
2 cups vegetable oil
1 cup Panko bread crumbs
1 cup unsweetened shredded coconut
1 lb large shrimp, peeled and deveined
Kosher salt, to taste
Freshly ground black pepper, to taste
1/2 cup all-purpose flour
2 large eggs, beaten
1 orange, cut into wedges, for garnish
Fresh cilantro sprigs, for garnish

Pineapple Sauce:
1 cup fresh pineapple, cut into chunks
1/8 cup brown sugar
1/8 cup white wine vinegar
2 tsp soy sauce
1 small garlic clove, minced
1/8 cup hoisin sauce
1/4 lemon, juice and zest
1/4 cup orange marmalade
1/4" piece fresh ginger, skin removed
1/8 habanero, de-seeded

Directions:

Lemon Shrimp:
In a large bowl, combine shrimp, lemon zest, salt, pepper, and thyme. Marinate in mixture for at least 30 minutes in the refrigerator.

Preheat oven to 400 degrees.

Line a baking sheet with aluminum foil. Place shrimp onto the prepared baking sheet. Place into oven and roast just until pink, firm, and cooked through, about 6 to 8 minutes.

Garnish with cilantro sprigs and orange wedges. Serve with lemon dipping sauce on the side.

Lemon Sauce:
In a saucepan, boil water and blanch yellow bell peppers until very tender, approximately 6 minutes. Strain the peppers.

In a blender, add peppers, lemon juice, and sugar. Purée until slightly smooth, then slowly add olive oil to emulsify, careful not to over blend or it will start to separate. Let cool and store in an airtight container. Refrigerate.

Coconut Shrimp:
In a large skillet over medium-high heat, heat vegetable oil.

In a large bowl, combine Panko bread crumbs and shredded coconut, and then set aside.

Season shrimp with salt and pepper to taste. Working one at a time, dredge shrimp in the flour, dip into the eggs, then dredge in the coconut mixture, pressing to coat.

Working in batches, add shrimp to the large skillet, and fry until evenly golden brown and crispy, about 2 to 3 minutes. Have a slotted spoon ready to remove shrimp from oil. Transfer to a paper towel-lined plate. Garnish with cilantro sprigs and orange wedges. Serve with pineapple dipping sauce on the side.

Pineapple Sauce:
In a blender, combine all ingredients and liquefy. Store in an airtight container and refrigerate.

Forrest docks his shrimp boat, the Jenny, in Lucy Point Creek in Lady's Island, South Carolina. The majority of the water scenes were filmed at Lucy Point, including the haul of shrimp Forrest and Lt. Dan bring in after the storm. Also situated along the creek is the private residence used to portray Bubba's mother's house. Today, Lady's Island is a residential area which was once used primarily for agriculture. The island is connected by bridges to Port Royal and Beaufort, the second-oldest city in SC, which offers scenic views and historic architecture.

A Box of Chocolates

"My mama always said life was like a box of chocolates.
You never know what you're gonna get."
- Forrest Gump from Forrest Gump

These handmade chocolate truffles are decorated with shredded coconut, mini chocolate chips, cocoa powder, and a scrumptiously crunchy nut topping! The truffles are then plated on a two-dimensional box created by a smooth chocolate drizzle. This box of chocolates is so sweet and delicious, you'll want to eat about a million-and-a-half of them!

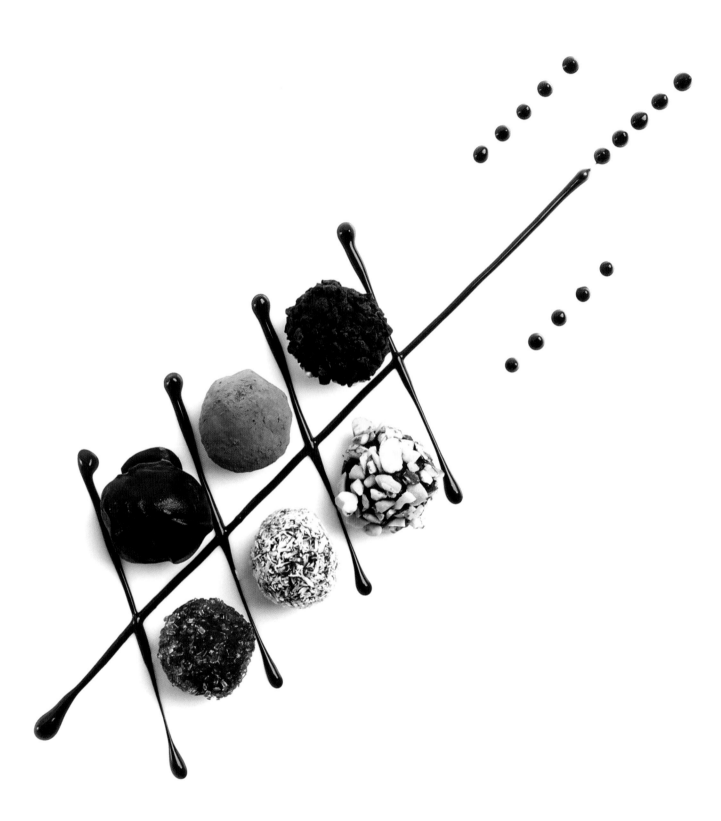

A Box of Chocolates

Hands-On: 1 hr
To Plate: 2 hrs 30 min
Serves: 4

Ingredients:

Chocolates:
10 oz semisweet chocolate, chopped
1/2 cup heavy cream
1 tbsp light corn syrup

Coating:
1/2 cup unsweetened cocoa powder
1/4 cup peanuts, crushed
1/4 cup shredded coconut
1/4 cup mini chocolate chips
10 oz semisweet chocolate, chopped

Directions:

Chocolates:
In a microwave safe bowl, heat the semisweet chocolate at 50% power for 30 seconds, stir, and repeat until melted.

In a small saucepan, heat heavy cream and corn syrup. Once the mixture is simmering, add to the melted chocolate. Let sit for 2 minutes and gently fold together until smooth. Line an 8-inch square pan with aluminum foil so that the bottom and sides are covered. Pour mixture into the pan and refrigerate for 1 hour.

Using a small scooper, scoop balls of chocolate out of the pan to form the truffles. Place them on a pan lined with foil and refrigerate for 30 minutes.

Coating:
In four small bowls, add each of the individual toppings.

In a microwave safe bowl, heat the semisweet chocolate at 50% power for 30 seconds, stir, and repeat until melted.

Remove truffles from the refrigerator. Using rubber gloves, dip them in the melted chocolate, and then dip them into your favorite coating. Best served at room temperature.

Place some of the leftover melted chocolate in a squeeze bottle and create a two-dimensional box on the plate for the chocolates prior to serving.

Mrs. Gump believes that destiny is what you make of it. She tells Forrest, "I happen to believe you make your own destiny. You have to do the best with what God gave you." She also says that "Life is like a box of chocolates. You never know what you're gonna get." Although Sally Field plays Forrest's mother, she is only 10 years older than Tom Hanks. Field played Hanks' love interest in the 1988 film *Punchline*.

THE VELVETY ROSE

"What? You think a first-class girl can't drink?"
–Rose DeWitt Bukater from Titanic

The Velvety Rose is based on the Black Velvet, a cocktail that's been enjoyed since 1861. The elegant flavor of the cocktail comes from the combination of the rich Irish stout and the crispness of the champagne. Legend has it that Heidsieck & Co. Monopole Blue Top Champagne was the official bubbly aboard the RMS Titanic. You'll never want to let it go.

Serves: 1

Ingredients:

3 oz Guinness Extra Stout, chilled
3 oz Heidsieck & Co. Monopole Blue
    Top (Non-Vintage) Champagne,
    chilled

Directions:

With your favorite Irish folk music
playing, slowly fill a champagne
flute with 3 onces of Guinness, and
then gently top with 3 ounces of
champagne.

Dance and be merry, but be careful
to not spill your drink!

SWEET PEA LAMB

"So, you gonna cut her meat for her, too, there, Cal?"
– Molly Brown from Titanic

This timeless recipe honors the elegance of the luxurious Titanic. Lamb with mint sauce was a part of the fifth course of the final dinner served in the first class dining saloon aboard the RMS Titanic on April 14, 1912. These tender and flavorful cuts of lamb are served with sweet peas, fava beans, and a fresh traditional mint sauce.

Sweet Pea Lamb

Hands-On: 45 min
To Plate: 6 hrs
Serves: 4

Ingredients:

Lamb:
1 fresh rosemary sprig, finely chopped
2 garlic cloves, crushed
Zest of 1 lemon
1 tsp crushed black pepper
2 tbsp olive oil
8 oz lamb loin
Salt, to taste
Freshly ground black pepper, to taste

Vegetable Garnish:
16 tiny new potatoes
Coarse sea salt, to taste
2 tbsp unsalted butter
1 cup sweet peas
1 cup fava beans

Mint Sauce:
1/2 cup red wine vinegar
1/2 avocado
1/2 cup mint, chopped
1/4 cup cilantro, chopped
Salt, to taste
Freshly ground black pepper, to taste
1/2 cup extra-virgin olive oil

Directions:

Lamb:
In a baking dish, combine the rosemary, garlic, lemon zest, crushed pepper, and olive oil. Add the lamb and rub the marinade on both sides of the meat. Cover and let marinate for at least 4 hours in the refrigerator.

Remove the lamb from the refrigerator about 1 hour before cooking.

Season the lamb with salt and pepper to taste, and grill it for about 5 minutes per side, depending on the thickness. Transfer to a plate, and let the lamb rest for 10 minutes.

Vegetable Garnish:
In a large pot of cold salted water, add the potatoes and bring to a boil. Cook until tender, about 15 minutes. Drain and set aside.

In a medium pot of boiling salted water, blanch the fava beans and sweet peas for 30 seconds, drain, and immediately transfer to a bowl of ice water to cool. Drain and set aside.

In a large skillet over low heat, melt the butter. Add the peas and cook for 1 minute, then add the potatoes and fava beans, stirring and tossing the vegetables until the potatoes are warmed through. Remove from heat and toss with 1 tablespoon of the mint sauce.

Mint Sauce:
In a blender, combine the vinegar, avocado, mint, cilantro, salt, and pepper. Blend until smooth, and then add the olive oil, a little at a time, to emulsify.

The ending of *Titanic* is intentionally left open to interpretation. The two most popular theories are that Rose is either dreaming, or that she has passed away in her sleep and that her soul is finally reunited with Jack and the others who lost their lives when the Titanic sank. If Rose has died, it fulfills Jack's prediction that she would die an old woman asleep in her bed.

The DUDE'S WHITE Russian

"Hey! Careful, man! There's a beverage here!"
- The Dude from The Big Lebowski

Sometimes, there's a drink that you can't go wrong with. Sometimes, the answer is simple. What would The Dude do? Well, before doing anything, he'd mix up his signature cocktail: a White Russian. The Dude can't abide without it. The finishing touch is the fella's rug coaster. It really brings the drink together!

Serves: 1

Ingredients:

2 oz half and half
1 oz Kahlúa
1 oz Smirnoff vodka

Directions:

In a cocktail shaker filled with ice, combine all ingredients. Shake vigorously until chilled, and then strain into a lowball glass filled with more ice.

Walter's BOWLING BALL Burger

"Those are good burgers, Walter."
- Donny from The Big Lebowski

Walter certainly cares about the rules. Although he can't roll on Shabbos, Walter can enjoy this meaty bowling ball-shaped burger. Why serve such a delicious burger on a bun when you can sit it on top of a crispy potato latke? Served with a savory apple sauce and some kosher pickle "pins", you'll have a meal that is definitely not "over the line!"

Walter's BOWLING BALL Burger

Hands-On: 50 min
To Plate: 1 hr 25 min
Serves: 4

Ingredients:

Potato Latkes:
2 1/2 lbs Yukon Gold potatoes, peeled
1 large white onion, finely minced
3/4 cup matzo meal
2 eggs, beaten
1 tbsp potato starch
1 1/4 tsp salt
1/2 tsp pepper
1 1/2 cups oil, for frying

Bowling Ball Burgers:
2 lbs ground beef
2 small garlic cloves, finely minced
2 tbsp parsley, chopped
2 eggs, beaten
2 tbsp bread crumbs
Kosher salt, to taste
Freshly ground pepper, to taste
8 bamboo skewers, for garnish
Kosher dill gherkin pickles, for garnish
4 cherry tomatoes, for garnish
Tofutti dairy-free sour cream
Chives, sliced, for garnish

Apple Lane Sauce:
1 tbsp extra-virgin olive oil
1 medium onion, diced
2 garlic cloves, finely minced
4 Granny Smith apples, peeled, cored, and roughly chopped
3 Roma tomatoes, diced
1/4 cup maple syrup
1/4 cup molasses
1/4 cup apple cider vinegar
2 tbsp fresh lemon juice
3 tbsp tomato paste
1 tbsp Worcestershire sauce
1 tsp kosher salt
1/2 tsp freshly ground black pepper
1 tsp coriander
1 tsp cumin
1 tsp smoked paprika
1 tsp mustard powder

Directions:

Potato Latkes:
Shred the potatoes and place them in a large bowl of cold water. Drain the grated potatoes and place them in a cheesecloth to help drain out as much of the water as possible.

In a large mixing bowl, combine the grated potatoes, onions, matzo meal, eggs, potato starch, salt, and pepper.

Preheat oven to 375 degrees.

In a large skillet over medium-high heat, heat 1/4 cup oil.

Scoop 3 tablespoons of the potato mixture, shape it into a disk, and carefully place in the hot oil. Fry latkes until brown and crispy, about 3 minutes per side. Remove from heat and place on a cooling rack.

Place cooled latkes on a baking sheet and cook through, about 10 minutes.

Bowling Ball Burgers:
In a large bowl, combine ground beef, garlic, parsley, eggs, bread crumbs, salt, and pepper.

Preheat oven to 400 degrees.

Shape meat mixture into four bowling ball-shaped burgers, size depending on your latkes.

Bake bowling ball burgers on a lightly oiled baking sheet until desired temperature, about 20 minutes.

To serve, place a bowling ball burger on a latke and top with a cherry tomato and a gherkin. Garnish the plate with Apple Lane Sauce, and a dollop of dairy-free sour cream sprinkled with chives.

Apple Lane Sauce:
In a large saucepan over medium heat, heat the oil. Add the onion, and sauté until translucent, about 8 minutes. Add the garlic and apples, and continue to cook over medium heat for 5 minutes, stirring often. Stir in the tomatoes, syrup, molasses, vinegar, lemon juice, tomato paste, Worcestershire sauce, salt, pepper, coriander, cumin, paprika, and mustard powder, and simmer until apples have softened, about 20 minutes.

In a blender, add apple mixture and blend until smooth.

Loyal fans were saddened when the shooting location for The Dude's favorite bowling alley, Hollywood Star Lanes, was torn down to be replaced by Kingsley Elementary School. A new bowling alley, Lucky Strike Hollywood, wanted to pay respect to the movie, so they purchased Lane 7 from Hollywood Star Lanes. It can now be found at Lucky Strike as a bar top.

BIG MOOSIE'S CHICKEN BREASTS

"Lost in oblivion, dark and silent and complete,
I found freedom."
- The Narrator from Fight Club

I am Jack's growling stomach. I get hungry, Jack gets distressed. Satisfy Jack's growling stomach and seek nourishing comfort with these big, juicy chicken breasts. The chicken is marinated with fresh lime juice, orange juice, cilantro, and a red chili pepper that adds a serious punch. Served with a zesty banana-mango salsa, black beans with garlic, and quinoa with red pepper and onion, this hearty meal is loaded with tasteosterone. Go ahead, you can cry.

BIG MOOSIE'S CHICKEN BREASTS

Hands-On: 25 min
To Plate: 55 min
Serves: 4

Ingredients:

Big Moosie's Chicken Breasts:
1 tsp cumin
3 cloves garlic
1 red chile, seeded
Pinch of black pepper
3/4 cup orange juice
The juice of 4 limes
1 tsp lime zest
1 tsp honey
1 tsp soy sauce
1/4 cup fresh cilantro
4 whole chicken breasts

Quinoa:
2 tbsp olive oil
1 onion, chopped
1 red pepper, chopped
1 1/2 cups dry quinoa
3 cups chicken stock

Black Beans:
2 tbsp olive oil
1 (15 oz) can black beans
2 cloves garlic, minced or grated
Salt, to taste
Pepper, to taste

Banana-Mango Salsa:
2 bananas, diced
1 mango, diced
1 small red onion, diced
1 red chile, seeded and chopped
1/2 lime, juiced
1/4 cup fresh cilantro, chopped
2 tbsp extra-virgin olive oil

Directions:

Big Moosie's Chicken Breasts:
In a blender, purée all ingredients except the chicken breasts. Pour the purée and the chicken into a zip-top bag and marinate for at least 20 minutes.

In a large skillet over medium-high heat, heat a drizzle of olive oil, then add the chicken breasts, and cook until cooked through, about 5 minutes per side.

To serve, cut the chicken breasts in half and serve with quinoa, beans, and salsa.

Quinoa:
In a large skillet over medium-high heat, add the oil and onion. Cook until the onion is soft, about 6 minutes. Add the red pepper, and quinoa, then cook until the red pepper is soft and the quinoa is lightly toasted, about 5 minutes. Pour in 3 cups of chicken stock, bring the mixture to a boil, cover, and then simmer until the quinoa is cooked and fluffy, about 25 to 30 minutes.

Black Beans:
In a saucepan over medium heat, add the olive oil, black beans, garlic, salt, and pepper. Cook until warmed through.

Banana-Mango Salsa:
In a bowl, add bananas, mango, red onion, red chile, lime juice, cilantro, and oil. Toss together until well incorporated.

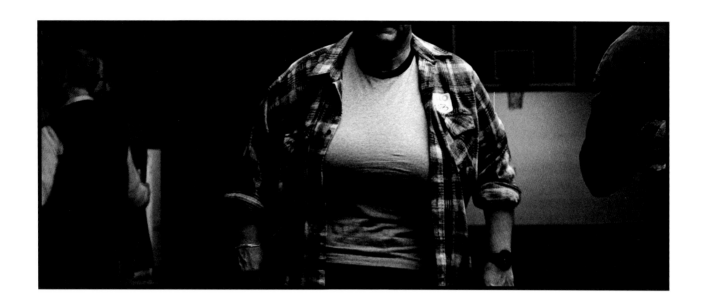

For his role in *Fight Club*, Meat Loaf wore a prosthetic fat suit to turn himself into the character of Bob. To ensure that his love handles and "man-boobs" would hang and move realistically, the fat suit was filled with bird seed. Because of this, the suit weighed about 100 pounds.

PAPER STREET CAKE CO.

"Soap. I make and I sell soap.
The yardstick of civilization."
- Tyler Durden from Fight Club

Fight Club was the beginning, now it's moved out of the basement and into the kitchen. What are we doing tonight? Tonight, we make cake. Using simple household ingredients, you too can make the yardstick of desserts. It's not made with liposuctioned fat, we promise. It's made with flour, creamy butter, and pink champagne. This dessert is sure to cause a little mayhem.

PAPER STREET CAKE CO.

Hands-On: 40 min
To Plate: 55 min
Serves: 4

Ingredients:

Cake:
12 tbsp unsalted butter, melted
1 1/2 cups sugar
2 tsp baking powder
2 cups all-purpose flour
1/4 tsp salt
6 large egg whites
1/4 cup milk
2 tsp vanilla extract
3/4 cup pink champagne

Frosting:
8 tbsp unsalted butter, room
 temperature
4 1/2 cups powdered sugar,
 divided
1/8 cup milk
1/8 cup pink champagne
1 tsp vanilla
Red food coloring

Directions:

Cake:
Preheat oven to 350 degrees.

In a bowl, combine butter, sugar, baking powder, flour, and salt.

In a large bowl, combine egg whites, milk, and vanilla. Slowly alternate incorporating the flour mixture and the champagne, 1/3 at a time, until fully mixed.

Grease a 9 x 9-inch cake pan, pour in the mixture, and bake until a toothpick inserted into the cake comes out clean, about 25 minutes. Allow the cake to fully cool before removing from the pan.

On a large cutting surface, lay the cake flat and cut out 3 1/2 x 2 1/2-inch rectangles.

Frosting:
In a bowl, combine butter, 2 cups of the sugar, milk, champagne, and vanilla, then slowly mix in the remaining sugar, and stir until you reach the desired consistency. Add red food coloring until you reach the desired pink color.

Gently apply frosting to each of the cakes and serve.

In order to enlighten The Narrator "to know, not fear, know, that someday" he's gonna die, Tyler teaches him a painful lesson. First, Tyler licks his lips and kisses the back of The Narrator's hand, leaving a kiss-shaped pattern. Then, he pours the lye. When lye comes into contact with water, it results in a violent chemical reaction, burning the part of the skin coated in saliva. Presumably, the same thing was done to Tyler at some point, leaving him with a kiss-shaped scar. It's only after The Narrator submits to the idea, and the searing pain, that Tyler relieves him of his agony. Vinegar neutralizes the chemical reaction and The Narrator comes away with a scar as a souvenir, and a new outlook on life.

Scotchy Scotch Scotch

"I love scotch. I love scotch. Scotchy Scotch Scotch,
here it goes down. Down into my belly."
– Ron Burgundy from Anchorman

You don't need an apartment full of leather-bound books that smell like rich mahogany in order to be a big deal. For the anchorperson that loves Scotch, we present the Scotchy Scotch Scotch: an aromatic cocktail comprised of ginger, honey syrup, lemon juice, and two types of Scotch. Staying classy has never been easier.

Serves: 1

Ingredients:

3 thin slices fresh ginger
2 oz blended Scotch whisky
3/4 oz lemon juice
3/4 oz honey syrup
1/4 oz single malt Scotch

Directions:

In a cocktail shaker, muddle ginger until well smashed. Add the Scotch, lemon juice, honey syrup, and ice.

Shake until chilled and strain into a lowball glass.

Top with the single malt Scotch and garnish with an orange slice, cocktail umbrella, and a swizzle stick, just to keep it classy.

Moonlight Lemonade

"Well, well, Lupin. Out for a little walk in the moonlight, are we?"
- Professor Snape from Harry Potter and the Prisoner of Azkaban

While there is no cure for lycanthropy, this potion can offer a solution for those who still wish to take a stroll in the moonlight without becoming a savage, bloodthirsty creature. Brewed with fresh lemonade, honey, lavender sugar, and dried peppermint, this magical mixture will charm your taste buds and cause even the most vicious of wolves to howl with delight. Professors, spike this concoction with a bit of vodka and a dash of lavender bitters to bewitch the mind, ensnare the senses, and maybe even cause a little mischief.

Serves: 1

Ingredients:

1 cup water
1 tsp lavender sugar
1 tsp dried peppermint leaves
2 tbsp honey
3 tbsp fresh-squeezed lemon juice
1/2 oz vodka
2 dashes lavender bitters
Maraschino cherry, for garnish
Lemon peel, for garnish

Directions:

In a small cauldron over medium-high heat, add the water, lavender sugar, and peppermint. Bring to a boil, remove from heat, and strain out the peppermint. Add in the honey and lemon juice, then stir until the honey has completely dissolved. Allow mixture to cool completely.

In a cocktail shaker with ice, add lemon mixture, vodka, and bitters. Shake vigorously until chilled, and strain into a glass. Garnish with a cherry and a lemon peel.

Omit the alcohol for a charming lavender lemonade.

Aldo's Smoky Mountain Scalps

*"Each and every man under my command
owes me one hundred Nazi scalps! And I want my scalps!"*
– Lt. Aldo Raine from Inglourious Basterds

This is a meal that's worthy of someone as legendary as the direct descendant of the mountain man Jim Bridger. The beef brisket is thoroughly rubbed with a bold blend of spices and slowly roasted until it's fall-apart tender. These smoky-sweet scalps of beef goodness are served with a zesty German potato salad that will have you parachuting behind enemy lines for more!

Aldo's Smoky Mountain Scalps

Hands-On: 40 min
To Plate: 4 hrs 30 min
Serves: 4

Ingredients:

Aldo's Smoky Mountain Scalps:

4 lbs beef brisket
2 cups beef stock
12 pearl onions
2 tbsp olive oil
Salt and pepper, to taste

Rub:

1/4 cup Dijon mustard
2 tbsp light brown sugar
2 tbsp granulated sugar
1 tbsp onion powder
1 tbsp garlic powder
2 tsp paprika
2 tsp chili powder
2 tsp kosher salt
1/2 tsp freshly ground black
   pepper

German Potato Salad:

2 lbs fingerling gold potatoes,
   cut in half
1/2 lb thick-cut bacon, rough
   chopped
3/4 cup finely chopped onion
1/3 cup white vinegar
1/4 cup sugar
2 tbsp whole grain mustard
1 tsp salt

Directions:

Aldo's Smoky Mountain Scalps:

Preheat oven to 350 degrees.

In a bowl, thoroughly mix all the rub ingredients together. Liberally season the brisket with the rub and place it in a roasting pan.

Roast the brisket uncovered for 1 hour. After an hour, add the beef stock and enough water to yield about 1/2 inch of liquid in the roasting pan. Lower the temperature to 300 degrees, seal the pan with foil, and continue roasting until the brisket is fork-tender, about 3 hours. Allow the roast to rest for at least 20 minutes before slicing.

In a bowl, toss the pearl onions in oil, and season with salt and pepper.

On a separate baking pan, add seasoned onions and roast until tender, about 45 minutes.

German Potato Salad:

In a medium-sized pot, add the potatoes and enough salted water to cover them by 2 inches. Bring the water to a boil, set temperature to medium-high and continue cooking until the potatoes are fork-tender, about 15 minutes.

In a large skillet over medium-high heat, fry the bacon until crisp. Pour off the fat, reserving about 1/4 cup in the pan. Lower the heat to medium, add the onion, and cook until translucent and light brown, about 4 to 5 minutes. Whisk in the vinegar, sugar, mustard, and salt. Add the cooked potatoes and toss to coat.

To serve, slice the brisket across the grain and serve with roasted onions and German potato salad.

It's fitting for the Basterds to scalp the Nazis as retribution for their cruelty towards Jews. Scalping is commonly associated with Native Americans, a group of people that were the subject of cruelty by those who colonized the Americas.

Landa's Apple
Strudel with Cream

"Wait for the cream."
– Hans Landa from Inglourious Basterds

Do you know what makes us such efficient hunters of desserts? Finding sweet and crispy treats is our specialty. That is a bingo! With hints of cinnamon, nutmeg, and dark rum, this fresh and crispy Austro-Hungarian dessert will delight any food connoisseur with its delicious apple filling. Don't forget the cream. How fun!

Landa's Apple Strudel with Cream

Hands-On: 40 min
To Plate: 1 hr 25 min
Serves: 4

Ingredients:

Strudel:
All-purpose flour
1 (17 oz) sheet puff pastry, thawed
5 Granny Smith apples
1/4 cup lemon juice
4 tbsp unsalted butter
1/2 cup granulated sugar
1/4 cup almonds, sliced
1 tsp ground cinnamon
1/2 tsp ground nutmeg
6 tbsp dark rum
1/4 cup apple juice
1 tbsp cornstarch
1 egg, beaten
Powdered sugar, for topping

The Cream:
1 cup heavy whipping cream
1 tbsp white sugar

Directions:

Strudel:
Preheat oven to 400 degrees.

On a lightly-floured work surface, unfold pastry and roll it out to a 12 x 14-inch rectangle. Line a baking sheet with parchment paper, place the pastry on the sheet, and refrigerate while making the filling.

Peel the apples and cut them into thick slices. Place the slices in a large bowl, add the lemon juice, and combine until the apples are all coated with the lemon juice.

In a large skillet over medium heat, melt the butter. Add apples, granulated sugar, almonds, cinnamon, and nutmeg. Increase heat to medium-high and cook, tossing occasionally, until apples are tender, about 15 minutes. Stir in the rum and apple juice, then slowly add cornstarch as needed to thicken slightly. Spread the filling onto a baking sheet to cool.

Remove the pastry from the refrigerator. Place a thick row of filling onto the pastry lengthwise, leaving a 1-inch border on each side. Fold the pastry over the filling and continue rolling the pastry until the seam side is down.

Brush pastry with egg. Using a knife, cut vents in center of pastry, and bake until golden brown, about 20 minutes.

Let rest 15 minutes before serving.

The Cream:
Chill a metal bowl in the freezer for 15 minutes.

In the chilled metal bowl, add cream and sugar, then using an electric mixer, whisk until stiff peaks form. Place in a piping bag prior to serving.

To serve, sprinkle the strudel with powdered sugar and top with a nice serving of the cream. Make sure to serve with a glass of milk!

During the chilling strudel scene in *Inglourious Basterds*, it's debatable whether or not Colonel Hans Landa knows Shosanna's real identity. He may not have seen her face during their first encounter at the LaPadite dairy farm, but given his reputation as "The Jew Hunter" and his meticulous detective work, he may have seen a photo or have a physical description of her. Landa ordering milk and cream for Shosanna may be an interrogation tactic to assert his superiority and to suggest to her that he knows her secret. Alternatively, he may not recognize her and the ordering of the milk and cream is a coincidence.

HAIR OF THE TIGER

*"To a night we'll never remember,
but the four of us will never forget!"
- Phil Wenneck from The Hangover*

Did you wake up this morning with a jungle cat in the bathroom? Missing a tooth? Or maybe there was a human baby in the closet? Somebody must have slipped a hangover into your drink last night. Relieve your suffering with the Hair of the Tiger that bit you. Known all over as the quintessential hangover cure, we've taken the Bloody Mary to a whole new level using carrot juice, orange juice, rye vodka, pickle brine, olive brine, fresh ginger, spices, and lots of pepper. Tigers love pepper. No cinnamon, though. Tigers hate cinnamon.

Serves: 1

Ingredients:

Hair of the Tiger:

1 orange wedge
1 tbsp Old Bay Seasoning, for
   glass rim
1 lime wedge
1/4" piece of fresh ginger, peeled
2 tsp raw sugar
2 oz rye vodka
1 tsp dried dill
1 tsp celery salt
1 tsp ground white pepper
1/2 tsp black pepper

Pinch of cayenne pepper
1 tsp prepared horseradish
2 dashes Worcestershire sauce
2 dashes hot sauce
1/2 oz pickle brine
1/4 oz olive brine
3 oz carrot juice
1 oz orange juice

Hangover Garnish:

1 slice thick-cut bacon, cooked
1 piece of smoked cheddar cheese
1 habanero pepper
1 olive

Directions:

Hair of the Tiger:

Moisten the outer rim of a
hurricane glass with an orange
wedge. Set aside the orange
wedge. Coat the moistened rim of the glass
with Old Bay Seasoning.

In a cocktail shaker, squeeze the
orange and lime wedges and drop
them in. Add the ginger and
raw sugar, then muddle all the
ingredients together. Add vodka,
dill, celery salt, white pepper,
black pepper, cayenne pepper,
horseradish, Worcestershire sauce,
hot sauce, pickle brine, olive brine,
carrot juice, orange juice, and then
fill with ice.

Shake until chilled. Strain and pour
into the rimmed glass.

Garnish drink with the slice of
thick-cut bacon, cube of cheese,
habanero pepper, and olive.

BERK'S BEER FLOAT

"This is Berk. It's twelve days north of Hopeless,
and a few degrees south of Freezing to Death.
It's located solidly on the Meridian of Misery."
– Hiccup from How to Train Your Dragon

On the Isle of Berk, the food is tasteless and tough, but luckily the ale is cold and stout! This hardy beverage is the perfect treat after a long day of dragon slaying. Just fill a tankard with two large scoops of vanilla ice cream and then top it off with a quality coffee stout and a drizzle of beer-infused chocolate syrup.

Serves: 1

Ingredients:

1 cup stout beer
1 cup sugar
1 cup cocoa powder
1 tsp vanilla extract
1/8 tsp salt
2 scoops vanilla ice cream
1 bottle Great Divide Espresso
    Oak Aged Yeti Stout beer

Directions:

In a saucepan, add 1 cup stout beer, sugar, cocoa powder, vanilla extract, and salt, then bring to a boil. Reduce heat to a simmer and allow to thicken, about 5 minutes. Set chocolate syrup aside and let cool.

Add 2 scoops of vanilla ice cream to a large mug. Pour Espresso Stout into the glass, allowing the ice cream to float to the top. Before serving, drizzle a little chocolate syrup over the ice cream. Place the remaining syrup in the refrigerator for future use.

Omit the alcohol for an enjoyable root beer float by replacing the 1 cup of stout beer in the syrup with 1 cup of water, and using root beer instead of the oak aged stout in the float.

THE KICK

"Give him the kick. Dunk him!"
– Arthur from Inception

To awaken Cobb out of his deep sleep and refresh his senses, he is given "the kick". Energize your senses with this invigorating bomb shot made from vodka, Aftershock Red, and a splash of lime, which is then dunked into your favorite energy drink. Once the energy has taken hold of the brain, it's almost impossible to eradicate.

Serves: 1

Ingredients:

1 can (250ml) Red Bull,
  chilled
3/4 oz vodka
3/4 oz Aftershock Red
1 splash of fresh lime juice

Directions:

Pour the Red Bull into a
standard highball glass.

In a cocktail shaker
with ice, add the vodka,
Aftershock Red, and
lime juice. Shake
vigorously until chilled,
and then strain into a
shot glass.

When you are ready to
drink, drop the shot,
glass and all, into the
highball glass with the
Red Bull. To get the full
effect, drink it quickly in
one shot.

INCEPTION TURDUCKEN

"You mustn't be afraid to dream a little bigger, darling."
— Eames from Inception

A dream within a dream within a dream is sweet pork sausage within a duck within a chicken within a turkey. Cut through the various layers of this massive poultry dish, and feast your eyes, and your face, on this beast of a meal that explodes with flavor on every level. Dream big, eat bigger.

INCEPTION TURDUCKEN

Hands-On: 1 hr 20 min
To Plate: 3 hrs 5 min
Serves: 4

Ingredients:

Turducken:
1 boneless, skinless turkey breast
1 boneless, skinless chicken
 breast
1 boneless, skinless duck breast
Salt, to taste
Pepper, to taste
2 cups Italian sausage, crumbled
1/2 cup Panko bread crumbs
3 cloves garlic
2 tbsp olive oil
2 cups carrots, diced
2 onions, diced
2 cups chicken stock

Paradox Potatoes:
4 large baking potatoes
2 tbsp unsalted butter, melted
Salt, to taste
Pepper, to taste
4 slices sharp cheddar cheese,
 cut into squares
4 slices white American cheese,
 cut into squares
4 slices bacon, cooked and
 chopped

Tarragon Cherry Sauce:
2 cups fresh cherries, pitted
2 tbsp fresh tarragon
3 garlic cloves, minced
1 cup dry red wine
1/2 cup chicken broth
2 tbsp unsalted butter

Tossed Spinach:
1 lb spinach
2 tbsp extra-virgin olive oil

Directions:

Turducken:
Preheat oven to 350 degrees.

On a large cutting board, lay down plastic wrap. Butterfly the three breasts. Place the butterflied turkey breast between two pieces of plastic wrap. Using the flat side of a meat hammer, pound the turkey until it is evenly flat, about 1/2-inch thick. Repeat this process for the chicken breast and duck breast.

Season each breast with salt and pepper. Place the chicken on top of the turkey, and the duck on top of the chicken, keeping the breasts as centered as possible.

In a bowl, combine the sausage, Panko, and garlic. Place a row of the sausage stuffing across the center of the top layer of the turducken (the duck) lengthwise. Because the breasts vary in size, you may have some stuffing left over, but do not overstuff the turducken.

Tightly roll the turducken together. Using cooking twine, truss the rolled meat widthwise leaving a space of no more than 2 inches between each knot. When you are done, create one knot lengthwise across the whole roll. Rub olive oil over the entire roll.

In a baking pan, add carrots, onions, and enough chicken stock to cover the bottom of the pan, about 1 cup. Place the rolled turducken in the pan, and bake until golden brown and the internal temperature reaches 165 degrees, about 2 hours.

Carefully baste after the first hour of baking. If the liquid in the pan runs dry, add more stock to cover the pan. Let rest for 20 minutes before slicing.

Serve sliced turducken with spinach, a potato, and garnish with the cherry sauce.

Paradox Potatoes:
Cut even slits across each potato widthwise nearly all the way through, but making sure to leave the bottom intact. Brush the cut potatoes with the melted butter, and season with salt and pepper.

On a baking tray, bake the potatoes for 30 minutes, brush on more butter, and bake an additional 40 minutes or until desired crispiness.

After removing potatoes from the oven, alternate toppings (cheddar cheese, American cheese, and bacon) between each slit.

Bake again until the cheese is melted, about 5 minutes.

Tarragon Cherry Sauce:
In a saucepan over medium heat, add the cherries, tarragon, and garlic, then cook while stirring for 1 minute. Stir in the wine and chicken broth, reduce heat, and simmer uncovered until sauce is reduced to 2 cups, about 5 minutes. Stir in butter and season with salt and pepper. Using a blender, purée the sauce and place it in a squeeze bottle for garnish.

Tossed Spinach:
In a large bowl, gently toss the spinach and oil together.

Dying under heavy sedation is not the only way to get to Limbo. As Cobb explains early on in *Inception*, a person can end up in Limbo by attempting to go too many dream levels deep. Limbo is not one person's dream, but a shared, unconstructed dream space. It contains anything left behind by someone sharing the dream who has been there before. Near the end of the film, Cobb and Ariadne find themselves in the once-pristine city created by Cobb and Mal.

Mad Hatter's Mad Tea

"Well, as you can see, we're still having tea.
And it's all because I was obliged to kill time
waiting for your return. You're terribly late, you know."
–The Mad Hatter from Alice in Wonderland

Don't be late for this very important date. Follow the White Rabbit down the rabbit hole and join us for tea! This maddeningly delicious concoction is made with Earl Grey tea, a touch of fresh lemon juice, a splash of vodka, a dash of lavender bitters, and is sweetened with honey-lavender syrup. Down with the bloody big head!

Serves: 1

Ingredients:

Mad Hatter's Mad Tea:

4 oz lavender Earl Grey tea,
   steeped and cooled
1 oz honey-lavender syrup
1/2 oz fresh lemon juice
1 1/2 oz vodka
3 dashes lavender bitters

Honey-Lavender Syrup:

1/2 cup water
1/2 cup honey
2 tbsp lavender buds

Directions:

Mad Hatter's Mad Tea:

In a cocktail shaker with ice, add tea, syrup, lemon juice, vodka, and bitters.

Shake vigorously until chilled, then strain into a tea cup.

Omit the alcohol for an enjoyable cup of tea.

Honey-Lavender Syrup:

In a small saucepan over medium-high heat, add water, honey, and lavender, then bring to a boil.

Stir, reduce heat, and simmer until the liquid reduces by about 1/3, about 20 minutes.

Strain out lavender, let cool, and pour into a jar with a lid until ready to use.

THE
MERMAN

"He had the conch in his hands!
I am never gonna see a merman. Ever."
- Hadley from The Cabin in the Woods

Dude, Hadley was right. Everything is cooler with a merman. So, let's get this party started! Blow the conch shell and summon this terrifyingly delicious mixture of pineapple juice, lemon-lime soda, a splash of Blue Curaçao, and silver tequila. Tequila is our lady! Our lady! You'll be glad you bet on this monster of a cocktail. Just be careful, the cleanup on them is a nightmare.

Serves: 1

Ingredients:

3 oz silver tequila
1 oz pineapple juice
2 oz lemon-lime soda
Splash of Blue Curaçao

Directions:

In a cocktail shaker with ice, add tequila and pineapple juice. Shake vigorously until chilled, and then strain into a glass. Top with lemon-lime soda and a splash of Blue Curaçao to achieve desired color.

VISHNU'S DELIGHT

"Thank you, Lord Vishnu. Thank you
for coming in the form of a fish
and saving our lives."
- Pi Patel from Life of Pi

Inspired by Pi's gift from the Hindu god Vishnu, this delectable mahi-mahi is bathed in a tangy lime marinade and then pan-seared to perfection. The orchid represents the lotus blossom that Vishnu holds. These gorgeous, edible flowers exude a delicate aroma that offers a fresh, crisp taste to the heavenly meal. The conch salad, served in an endive "life boat", is a tribute to Panchajanya, the sacred conch shell that Vishnu also holds. It's a truly delicious meal, regardless of which story you wish to believe.

VISHNU'S DELIGHT

Hands-On: 25 min
To Plate: 2 hrs 40 min
Serves: 4

Ingredients:

Mahi-Mahi:

1 1/2 cups extra-virgin olive oil
2 cloves garlic, minced
1/4 tsp ground black pepper
1 tsp cayenne pepper
2 pinches salt
1/4 cup lime juice
1/4 tsp lime zest
4 (4 oz) fresh mahi-mahi fillets
4 white orchids, for garnish

Conch Salad:

1 lb cleaned fresh conch, diced
1/4 cup fresh orange juice
2 tbsp fresh lime juice
2 tbsp fresh lemon juice
1 jalapeño pepper, stemmed,
  seeded and minced
2 tbsp extra-virgin olive oil
1 tbsp kosher salt
1 tbsp fresh cilantro leaves,
  chopped
1/2 cucumber, peeled and
  minced
1/2 yellow bell pepper, minced
1/2 red bell pepper, minced
1/4 red onion, minced
1/2 cup fresh tomato, diced
Endives, for serving

Mousseline Sauce:

1/2 cup heavy whipping cream
3 egg yolks
16 tbsp unsalted butter, melted
2 tbsp fresh lemon juice
Salt and white pepper, to taste

Directions:

Mahi-Mahi:

In a mixing bowl, whisk the extra-virgin olive oil, minced garlic, black pepper, cayenne pepper, salt, lime juice, and lime zest. Place the mahi-mahi fillets in the mixture and marinate for at least 15 minutes.

In a skillet over medium-high heat, cook the fillets until the fish is lightly browned and flakes easily with a fork, about 3 minutes per side.

Serve mahi-mahi with conch salad, and garnish with the Mousseline sauce and a fresh white orchid.

Conch Salad:

In a large mixing bowl, combine all of the ingredients except the tomato and endives. Stir then refrigerate for at least 2 hours. Before serving, fold in the tomato. Place a serving of conch salad on top of an endive "lifeboat".

Mousseline Sauce:

Using an electric mixer, whip the heavy cream until stiff peaks form.

In a small saucepan over low heat, whisk the egg yolks. Continue whisking the eggs while slowly adding the melted butter until well incorporated, thick, and glossy. Whisk in lemon juice, salt, and pepper. Remove from heat and gently fold in the whipped cream.

Sauce is best used within 10 minutes of preparation and at room temperature.

In the most obvious of his hidden depictions in *Life of Pi*, Vishnu's sleeping form can be seen in the shape of the floating carnivorous island. At the beginning of the movie, we hear the adult Pi say, "Vishnu sleeps, floating on the shoreless cosmic ocean, and we are the stuff of his dreaming."

PI'S PIE

"I am Piscine Molitor Patel. Known to all as Pi,
the sixteenth letter of the Greek alphabet."
- Pi Patel from Life of Pi

This circular delight is inspired by Piscine's self-proclaimed nickname after the sixteenth letter of the Greek alphabet, which also represents the ratio of any circle's circumference to its diameter. The curd filling of Pi's Pie is made with Greek yogurt and mango, the national fruit of India. A great dessert can change everything you thought you knew about yourself.

PI'S PIE

Hands-On: 50 min
To Plate: 12 hrs
Serves: 4

Ingredients:

Pi's Pie Crust:
1 1/4 cup all-purpose flour
1 tbsp sugar
1/4 tbsp salt
8 tbsp unsalted butter, chilled,
    cut into 1/2" cubes
3 tbsp ice water

Mango Filling:
3 large ripe mangoes, peeled and
    pitted
1/3 cup sugar
3 tbsp fresh lime juice
Pinch of salt
4 large egg yolks
1 1/2 tsp powdered gelatin
4 tbsp unsalted butter, cut into
    small pieces
1 cup organic plain Greek
    yogurt
Fresh blueberries, for garnish

Berry Sauce:
1 cup fresh blueberries
8 tsp white sugar
1 tsp corn starch
1/4 cup water

Directions:

Pi's Pie Crust:
In a mixing bowl, combine flour, sugar, and salt. Work the butter into the flour until the mixture looks like a coarse meal. Add in ice water and combine. The mixture should come together like a ball. Add more ice water if the mixture is too dry. Form the dough into a disk, cover tightly with plastic wrap, and chill, about 1 hour.

Preheat oven to 400 degrees.

On a floured work surface, use a floured rolling pin to roll the dough into four disks, each slightly larger than a 4-inch tart pan.

In each of the four tart pans, carefully place the dough, trimming off the excess. Prick the bottom of the dough with a fork to prevent the dough from puffing up and bake until lightly browned, about 15 minutes. Set aside to cool.

Mango Filling:
In a food processor, purée mango, sugar, lime juice, and salt.

In a small bowl, combine the gelatin with 2 tablespoons of water.

Add the yolks and the gelatin mixture to the purée and continue to process. Place the mango purée in a metal bowl.

In a double boiler, whisk purée until a thermometer reaches about 175 degrees, about 10 minutes.

Remove bowl from heat and slowly whisk in butter. Gently stir in Greek yogurt, cover, and allow to cool at room temperature. Pour mixture into the prepared pie crust and refrigerate overnight.

Create the Pi symbol in the middle of Pi's Pie with the blueberry sauce, garnish with blueberries, and enjoy!

Berry Sauce:
In a small saucepan, combine the blueberries, sugar, and cornstarch, and bring to a boil. Reduce heat and simmer for 5 minutes. Then remove from heat and let cool. The sauce will begin to thicken.

In a blender, purée the sauce, strain it to remove the seeds, and pour the smooth mixture into a squeeze bottle.

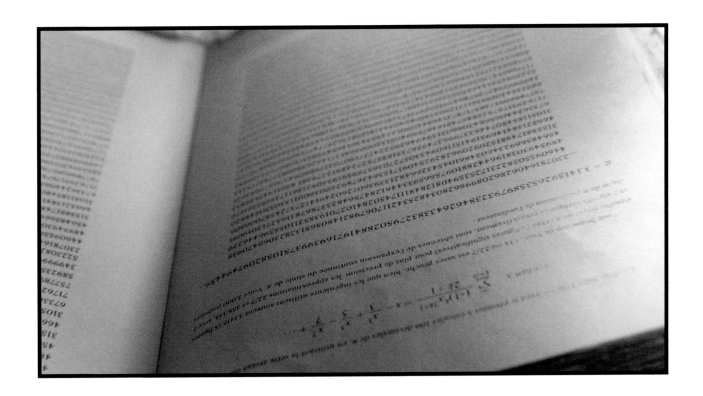

It is significant that Pi renames himself after the number representing the ratio of a circle's circumference to its diameter. Pi is an irrational number, meaning that it cannot be expressed as a simple fraction -- only approximated. In its decimal form, pi is infinite with no repeating patterns of numbers. The nature of the number could be interpreted as a metaphor for the nature of Pi's character.

Pot Brownies

"Oh, hey, listen. Try this.
I told my weed guy to step it up and he gave me that."
– Ted from Ted

Jonesing for something chocolate? Oh, hey, listen. Try this. We told our chef to step it up and he gave us this dessert. You're sure to get your sugar high on while enjoying this pot brownie... flower pot-shaped brownie, that is! It's actually pretty mellow and delicious. Make extra so your best bud, teddy bear or otherwise, doesn't bogart all your rich, chocolatey goodness. Go on, eat it up!

Pot Brownies

Hands-On: 15 min
To Plate: 1 hr 15 min
Serves: 4

Ingredients:

Pot Brownies:
Cooking spray
4 large eggs
1 cup brown sugar, sifted
1 cup granulated sugar, sifted
16 tbsp unsalted butter, melted
1 1/4 cups cocoa powder, sifted
1 1/2 tsp vanilla extract
1/2 cup flour, sifted
1/2 tsp salt
Cocoa powder, for garnish
Mint ice cream
Fresh mint leaves, for garnish

Chocolate Drizzle:
1/2 cup chocolate chips

Directions:

Pot Brownies:
Preheat oven to 325 degrees.

Spray flower pot cake pan molds with cooking spray.

In a mixer fitted with a whisk attachment, beat eggs at medium speed until fluffy. Add sugars, butter, cocoa powder, vanilla, flour, and salt, then continue to mix until well combined. Do not overmix.

Pour batter into prepared molds, only about 3/4 full. Bake for 25 minutes. Lower oven temperature to 300 degrees, then loosely cover pan with foil. Continue to bake until a toothpick inserted into the brownie comes out clean, about 20 more minutes.

When brownies are completely cooled, remove them from the molds and trim off excess from the tops so they look more like flower pots. Sift cocoa powder onto brownies.

Serve each Pot Brownie with a large scoop of mint ice cream, drizzle with chocolate, and garnish with a fresh mint leaf.

Chocolate Drizzle:
In a microwave safe bowl, heat the chocolate at 50% power for 30 seconds, stir, and repeat until melted.

Smoke it, vape it, dab it, or eat it. Marijuana use has come a long way from the traditional rolled up joint. With so many strains and ways to consume it, pot smokers have become more creative in obtaining the ultimate high. Amongst this mary-multitude, edibles have gained popularity because of the way they are metabolized, resulting in a more intense high. Move over kale, these greens are the new super "high" food.

SUGAR RUSH MILKSHAKE

"What's going on in this candy-coated Heart of Darkness?"
- Wreck-It Ralph from Wreck-It Ralph

Would you care for something sweet? Enjoy this frosty treat and have some candy! This whimsically creamy pink cotton candy milkshake is served in a candy-coated glass and topped with lollipops, Sour Patch Kids, jelly beans, cinnamon sticks, and sour balls. Get a little 'wrecked' by adding cotton candy vodka to the milkshake!

Serves: 1

Ingredients:

Vanilla frosting
Rainbow sprinkles
1/4 cup whole milk
1 cup vanilla ice cream
3 tbsp pink cotton candy sugar
   granules
2 oz cotton candy vodka
Lollipops
Sour Patch Kids
Jelly beans
Cinnamon sticks
Gummy worms
Green sour balls

Directions:

Spread vanilla frosting on the outside of a glass, about 1/3 of the way down. Apply rainbow sprinkles onto the frosting, and then place the glass in the freezer to set, about 10 minutes.

In a blender, add the milk, ice cream, cotton candy sugar, and vodka. Blend until smooth.

Remove the candy-coated glass from the freezer and carefully pour in the milkshake. Garnish with a collection of your favorite candies.

Omit the alcohol for an enjoyable milkshake.

AZOFF'S FISHBOWL

"You cleaning your fishbowl?"
– Donnie Azoff from The Wolf of Wall Street

Listen up! On new issue day, you better be on point! Azoff's Fishbowl is a fruity spiked punch made with vodka, rum, and fruit juices. It comes complete with Nerds candy gravel and a Swedish "goldfish". After you've sealed the deal, you have permission to clean out this fishbowl, just make sure you don't wear your geeky Mr. Rogers bowtie!

Serves: 4

Ingredients:

1 cup Nerds candy
5 oz vodka
5 oz Malibu rum
3 oz Blue Curaçao
6 oz sweet-and-sour mix
16 oz pineapple juice
16 oz lemon-lime soda
4 Swedish gummy fish

Directions:

Sprinkle the Nerds candy equally into four small fishbowls (or one 1/2-gallon fishbowl for a real party!) as "gravel".

Fill the bowls with ice.

In a pitcher, add the remaining ingredients (except for the gummy fish). Stir, and carefully pour the punch into the bowls. Drop a gummy fish into each bowl, and serve with straws.

8-Balls and Lemons

"Into the donuts, I see."
- Aunt Emma from The Wolf of Wall Street

Let us tell you something. Some will have you believe that there is no nobility in poverty, but when life gives you lemons, you make donuts. These confectionary delights are sweetened with a little powder (powdered sugar, that is) and topped with a hint of lemon zest. They're so delicious, it's hard to believe that they're legal. Enjoy responsibly!

8-Balls
and Lemons

Hands-On: 10 min
To Plate: 25 min
Serves: 4

Ingredients:

Donuts:

1/3 cup granulated sugar
4 tbsp unsalted butter, softened
1 large egg
1/3 cup milk
1 cup all-purpose flour
1 tsp baking powder
1/4 tsp kosher salt
1/4 tsp cinnamon
1 tbsp lemon zest
Cooking Spray

Topping:

3 tbsp unsalted butter, melted
3/4 cup powdered sugar
1 tbsp lemon zest, for garnish

Directions:

Donuts:

Preheat oven to 350 degrees.

In a large bowl, combine sugar and butter. Add the egg, milk, flour, baking powder, salt, cinnamon, and lemon zest. Continue mixing until well blended, about 2 minutes.

Spray a mini muffin pan with cooking spray. Add 1 tablespoon of mixture into each muffin cup, and bake until a toothpick inserted into a donut comes out clean, about 15 minutes. Allow to cool completely before removing from pan.

Dip each donut into the melted butter and roll in powdered sugar. Garnish with lemon zest.

In *The Wolf of Wall Street*, the actors are snorting crushed vitamin B tablets, not real cocaine. Although the substance is relatively harmless to snort, the actors reported that it burned their nostrils. In movies, if multiple takes are required when filming scenes involving fake cocaine, the prop master will often line the inside of the snort tube with Vaseline, which will pick up most of the powder before it reaches the nose.

IT'S ALL
ABOUT THE ROSÉ

*"Okay. I was at a wine tasting with my cousin Ernesto,
which was mainly reds, and you know I don't love reds,
man, you know? But there was a rosé that saved the day,
it was delightful."*
– Luis from Ant-Man

Show off your mad wine-pairing skills with this "crazy stupid fine" dinner! We got ginger-soy pork loin. We got bacon-wrapped dates stuffed with Parmesan cheese. We got grilled peach crostini with ricotta and prosciutto. Daaaaamn! And they all go mad-well with the delightful rosé! This charcuterie will really save the day!

IT'S ALL ABOUT THE ROSÉ

Hands-On: 45 min
To Plate: 7 hrs 10 min
Serves: 4

Ingredients:

Pork Loin:
1 (1 1/2 lb) boneless pork loin roast
1/2 cup soy sauce
1 tsp ground ginger
3 garlic cloves, finely minced
1 tbsp olive oil

Bacon-Wrapped Dates:
12 dates
1/4 lb block Parmesan cheese
12 strips bacon, thinly sliced

Grilled Peach Crostini:
1 French baguette
8 tbsp ricotta cheese
8 slices prosciutto
2 large peaches, sliced
Honey, for drizzling

Assembly:
1 bottle dry rosé, chilled, for serving
1 bunch green grapes
Parmesan cheese
Blackberries
Redcurrants
Fresh herbs, for garnish

Directions:

Pork Loin:
Trim the pork tenderloin of any excess fat and skin.

In a small bowl, add the soy sauce, ginger, and garlic. Whisk well to combine. In a gallon size zip-top bag, place pork tenderloin and soy sauce mixture, then seal the bag. Refrigerate for 6 hours, swishing around the contents of the bag half way through. Remove the tenderloin from the bag and discard the marinade. Allow the tenderloin to come to room temperature.

Preheat oven to 350 degrees.

In a cast-iron skillet over medium-high heat, heat the olive oil and add the tenderloin. Evenly brown all sides of the tenderloin and place the skillet in the oven. Cook until the internal temperature reaches 160 degrees, about 20 minutes. Allow the pork to rest 10 minutes before slicing.

Bacon-Wrapped Dates:
Preheat oven to 400 degrees.

Using a paring knife, cut a small slit across the length of each date, remove the pit, and replace it with a sliver of the Parmesan cheese. Reserve the rest of the cheese for serving. Wrap a slice of bacon around each of the stuffed dates.

On a baking sheet, place the wrapped dates and bake until golden brown and crispy, about 25 minutes.

Grilled Peach Crostini:
Using a bread knife, cut the baguette into thin slices.

On a hot grill, cook the baguette slices and peaches until grill marks are visible. Spread a tablespoon of ricotta onto each baguette slice, then top with a slice of prosciutto and a peach slice. Drizzle with honey before serving.

Assembly:
Serve the sliced tenderloin with a glass of rosé, bacon-wrapped dates, grilled peach crostini, grapes, Parmesan cheese (leftover from dates), blackberries, redcurrants, and fresh herbs. While you enjoy this delightful dinner, be sure to have a sip of rosé before trying each item. Think about how the wine complements the various flavors of each element of the meal.

186

Ant-Man's Scott Lang isn't the only superhero in the Marvel Cinematic Universe who started out on the wrong side of the law. In the comic books, Clint Barton (Hawkeye) was mistaken for a thief on his first day as a crime fighter. Natasha Romanoff (Black Widow) was a Russian spy and enemy of SHIELD. The Hulk's tragic and destructive history easily puts them all to shame.

CRAZY STUPID FINE WAFFLES

"You want some waffles?"
– Luis from Ant-Man

Let us give you a tip. It's airtight, like, super legit! When you're planning a heist, you gotta keep your friends fed. It's really important and stuff! So, are you the waffle aficionado of your crew? Whip up these crazy fine... like, fine fine... like, "crazy stupid fine" banana-apricot waffles. Topped with ricotta-mascarpone mousse and drizzled with a sublime amaretto-apricot syrup, this "crazy stupid fine" dessert is sure to get your friends really excited and stuff!

CRAZY STUPID FINE WAFFLES

Hands-On: 35 min
To Plate: 2 hrs 45 min
Serves: 4

Ingredients:

Waffles:
Cooking spray
1 (15 oz) can apricot halves,
  drained and chopped
1 cup unbleached flour
1 cup spelt flour
2 tsp baking powder
1/2 tsp kosher salt
1 tbsp granulated sugar
1/4 tsp cinnamon
1/4 tsp nutmeg
1 large overripe banana,
  chopped
1 large egg
1/2 tsp vanilla extract
1 cup buttermilk
1 cup whole milk
4 strawberries, thinly sliced, for
  garnish

Ricotta-Mascarpone Mousse:
1 cup heavy cream
1 lb ricotta cheese
8 oz mascarpone cheese
1/2 cup granulated sugar
Zest of 1 lemon

Amaretto-Apricot Syrup:
1 (15 oz) can apricot halves,
  drained, and chopped
1 1/2 cups packed dark brown
  sugar
1/4 tsp kosher salt
1 1/4 cups water
1/4 cup amaretto
1 1/2 tsp ginger, freshly grated

Directions:

Waffles:
Preheat a waffle iron and grease with cooking spray.

In a blender, purée the apricots.

In a large mixing bowl, sift together the unbleached flour, spelt flour, baking powder, salt, sugar, cinnamon, and nutmeg.

In a bowl, mash the banana and add the egg, vanilla, buttermilk, milk, and puréed apricots, then combine.

In the bowl of an electric mixer, combine the dry ingredients with the wet ingredients, and blend into a smooth batter.

Pour batter onto the hot waffle iron, making sure not to overfill, and cook until golden brown, about 5 minutes.

Top each waffle with mousse and a thinly sliced strawberry. Serve with amaretto-apricot syrup.

Ricotta-Mascarpone Mousse:
In a medium bowl, beat the cream until soft peaks form.

In a large bowl, add the ricotta, mascarpone, sugar, and lemon zest. Blend until smooth. Gradually fold the whipped cream into the ricotta, cover, and refrigerate for 2 hours.

Amaretto-Apricot Syrup:
In a medium saucepan over high heat, add the apricots, sugar, salt, water, amaretto, and ginger, then bring to a boil. Reduce heat and simmer, stirring occasionally, until apricots have softened, about 5 minutes. Mash with a potato masher and continue to simmer until the mixture has reduced by 1/3, about 15 minutes. Strain into a heatproof bowl and discard the solids. Discard any foam off the surface and allow the mixture to cool.

The Milgrom Hotel, where Scott Lang, Luis, and the rest of the crew live, is named after comic book artist Al Milgrom. The exterior of the Milgrom is actually the Riviera Hotel on the corner of Jones and Ellis in San Francisco. The Riviera Hotel was built around 1907 as a luxury hotel, but now serves as a low-income housing hotel.

The Contract

"Oh, I exercise control in all things, Miss Steele."
- Christian Grey from Fifty Shades of Grey

The following are the terms of a binding cocktail contract between the Dominant and the Submissive ingredients. The fundamental purpose of this contract is to allow the imbiber to explore alcohol safely, with due respect and regard for his or her limits, enjoyment, and well-being. The Dominant ingredients are as follows: bourbon and bitters. The sweet cherries are the Submissive. The cherries are slowly muddled, gently shaken with the red vermouth and Dominant elements, then strained into a chilled glass. You'll like it, we promise.

Serves: 1

Ingredients:

8 dark pitted cherries
2 oz bourbon whiskey
3/4 oz sweet red vermouth
4 drops Angostura bitters

Directions:

In a cocktail shaker, add the cherries
and muddle them to a juicy pulp.

Add the whiskey, vermouth, bitters,
and ice, then gently shake. Strain
into a chilled champagne saucer.

Bondage Bird

"Okay... rope, tape, cable ties.
You're the complete serial killer."
- Anastasia Steele from Fifty Shades of Grey

Obey Mr. Grey and feed your inner goddess. This bondage bird will pleasure your senses and awaken your taste buds to a world of tantalizing flavor. The tender, succulent chicken breasts are seductively seasoned, slowly stuffed, and then gently bound with twine. The chicken is accompanied by baked figs and sautéed cherries, creating a masterpiece of a meal that your partner won't soon forget. Laters, baby.

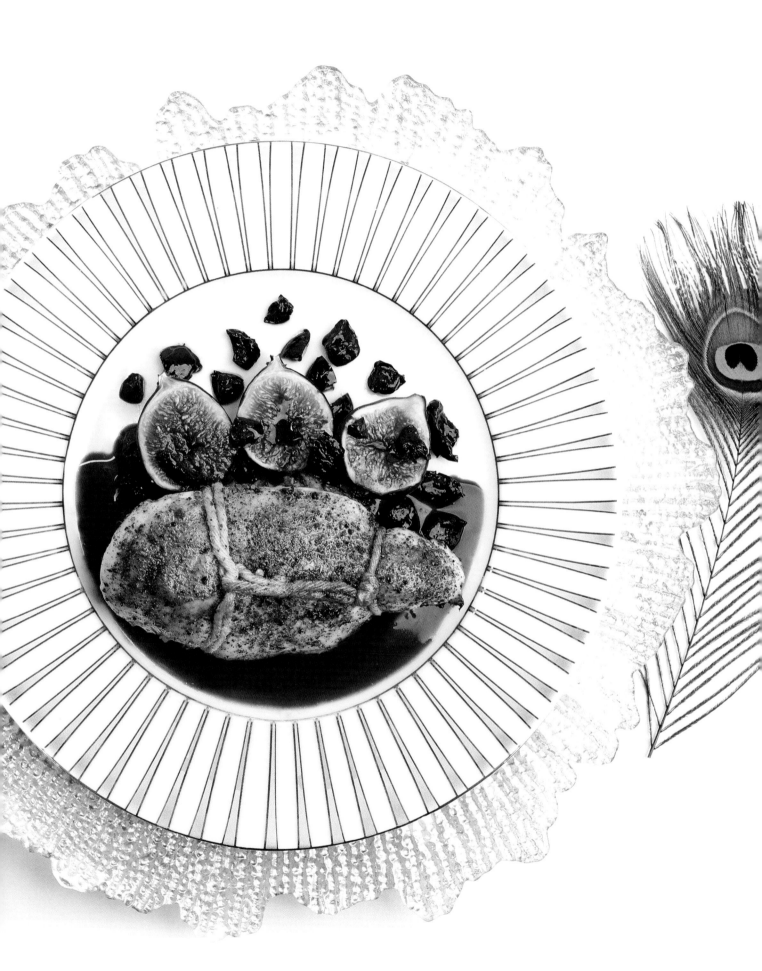

Bondage Bird

Hands-On: 50 min
To Plate: 1 hr 35 min
Serves: 4

Ingredients:

Bondage Bird:

1/2 lb sweet Italian sausage
1 cup fresh baby spinach, finely
    chopped
1 small white onion, minced
1 garlic clove, minced
1/4 cup sun-dried tomatoes
1/4 cup grated Parmigiano-
    Reggiano cheese
2 tbsp salt
1 tsp peppercorns
1/2 tsp allspice berries
1/2 tsp juniper berries
5 cloves
4 bay leaves
4 garlic cloves, minced
4 boneless chicken breasts, cut
    in half lengthwise

Racy Red Wine Sauce:

2 shallots, finely sliced
2 cups cherries, pitted and
    halved
2 tbsp olive oil
3/4 cup dry red wine
1 tbsp finely shredded orange
    zest
2 tbsp sugar
2 tbsp fresh orange juice
Salt, to taste

Feisty Figs:

12 ripe figs
Fresh thyme sprigs
Olive oil
Racy Red Wine Sauce, for
    brushing

Directions:

Bondage Bird:

Remove the casing from sausage and place it in a mixing bowl. Mix in spinach, onion, garlic, sun-dried tomatoes, Parmigiano-Reggiano, and salt.

Preheat the oven to 400 degrees.

In a grinder, grind the peppercorns, allspice, juniper, cloves, and bay leaves. Mix the ground spices with the salt and add the garlic. Season the breasts on all sides with the spice mixture. Add a couple tablespoons of the sausage mixture into each of the breasts and, using butcher's twine, tie each breast back together.

On an oiled roasting pan, roast the chicken breasts until golden brown and the internal temperature reaches 165 degrees, about 15 minutes each side. Remove the chicken from the oven and let rest for 10 minutes before slicing.

Racy Red Wine Sauce:

In a skillet over medium-high heat, sauté sliced shallots and cherries in olive oil until shallots begin to brown. Mix in red wine, orange zest, sugar, orange juice, and salt. Cook, stirring often, until liquid reduces by half, about 10 minutes. Set aside 4 tablespoons of the cherry mixture for garnish.

In a blender, purée the sauce mixture. Strain and pour red wine sauce into a squeeze bottle.

Feisty Figs:

Split the figs in half from top to bottom, through the stem.

On a baking sheet, arrange several sprigs of thyme and place the figs, cut side up, over the thyme sprigs. Drizzle olive oil and some red wine sauce over each fig. Bake the figs at 400 degrees until juicy, about 20 minutes.

Serve chicken with figs, red wine sauce, and garnish each plate with a tablespoon of cooked cherries.

The sex scenes in Christian's Red Room were all filmed during the final week of production so that Dakota Johnson and Jamie Dornan were comfortable with each other. The set was closed, meaning only the people that absolutely needed to be there were present. Two cameras were used whenever possible to reduce the number of takes, and the scenes were shot from a distance with the same techniques wildlife photographers use to keep from scaring the animals, including using remote controlled cameras.

BLOOD AND SNOW

*"Bringing desperate men in alive
is a good way to get yourself dead."
- Major Marquis Warren from The Hateful Eight*

The Blood and Snow is the perfect cocktail companion for this epic tale of bloodshed in a blizzard. Rye whiskey, blood orange juice, cherry liqueur, sweet vermouth, Grand Marnier, and Angostura bitters are shaken and then poured over a mound of crushed ice. Before serving, the cocktail is drizzled with a deliciously bloody blood orange syrup. Each sip of this frozen drink will taste like sweet freedom to a murderous outlaw destined for the noose.

Serves: 1

Ingredients:

Blood and Snow:

1 1/2 oz rye whiskey
3 oz fresh blood orange juice
2 oz Cherry Heering
1 oz sweet vermouth
1/2 oz Grand Marnier
1 dash Angostura bitters
Crushed ice

Blood Orange Syrup:

2 tbsp blood orange zest
2 tbsp orange juice
3 blood oranges, peeled and
   pith removed
1/2 cup sugar
2 tbsp blackberry preserves

Directions:

Blood and Snow:

In a cocktail shaker with ice, add the rye whiskey, blood orange juice, Cherry Heering, vermouth, Grand Marnier, and bitters, then shake.

Pour a quarter of the mixture into the glass and top with a mound of crushed ice.

Drizzle the blood orange syrup over the ice and then carefully pour more of the whiskey mixture into the glass.

Blood Orange Syrup:

In a medium saucepan, combine orange zest, orange juice, and peeled blood oranges, then bring to a boil. Reduce heat to a simmer and cook until oranges collapse, about 10 minutes.

Strain mixture, return liquids to the saucepan, and discard the solids. Add sugar and blackberry preserves, then return to a boil. Reduce heat to a simmer and continue to cook mixture until syrupy, about 5 minutes.

Allow the syrup to cool completely before serving.

BLOODY TART

"When you get to hell, John, tell 'em Daisy sent you."
– Daisy Domergue from The Hateful Eight

This here is the Bloody Tart, a good and gory mocha dessert that all happens around a daisy. The buttery Oreo crust holds a filling made with dark brewed coffee (of the non-poisonous variety), dark chocolate, and a hint of Grand Marnier. Served with marinated blood oranges and splattered with blood orange syrup, this dessert is sure to sweeten up any shootout.

BLOODY TART

Hands-On: 35 min
To Plate: 2 hrs 45 min
Serves: 4

Ingredients:

Mocha Tarts:
2 cups finely ground Oreo
   cookies, cream removed
10 tbsp unsalted butter, melted
3 tbsp brewed dark coffee,
   divided
1 1/4 cups heavy cream
2 tbsp Grand Marnier
12 oz dark chocolate chips
2 large eggs, beaten
1/4 tsp kosher salt
4 daisies, for garnish

Blood Orange Syrup:
2 tbsp blood orange zest
2 tbsp orange juice
3 blood oranges, peeled and pith
   removed
1/2 cup sugar
2 tbsp blackberry preserves
16 blood orange wedges

Directions:

Mocha Tarts:
Preheat oven to 350 degrees.

In a bowl, combine ground cookies, melted butter, and 1 tablespoon of the coffee. Press mixture into four 4-inch tart pans. Bake for 10 minutes, remove from the oven, and allow to cool completely before filling.

In a saucepan, bring the cream to a boil. Remove from heat, stir in the remaining 2 tablespoons of the brewed coffee and the Grand Marnier. Add the chocolate chips and let sit in the mixture undisturbed for 5 minutes, then stir together until smooth.

In a bowl, combine the eggs, salt, and vanilla. Pour into the chocolate mixture, and stir until completely combined. Pour mixture into the cooled tart shells and bake until the filling is set along the edges but still soft in the very center, 15 to 20 minutes. Remove from oven and refrigerate until set, about 2 hours. Serve each tart with Blood Orange Syrup and garnish with a daisy.

Blood Orange Syrup:
In a medium saucepan, combine orange zest, orange juice, peeled blood oranges, and bring to a boil. Reduce heat to a simmer and cook until oranges collapse, about 10 minutes. Strain mixture, return liquids to the saucepan, and discard the solids. Add sugar and blackberry preserves, then return to a boil. Reduce heat to a simmer, add the blood orange wedges, and cook for 5 minutes. Allow the syrup to completely cool before serving.

In *The Hateful Eight*, the stagecoach that John Ruth, Major Warren, and Daisy ride in is owned by the Butterfield Overland Stage Company. Butterfield is the same name that appears on the stagecoach in 1957's *3:10 to Yuma*. Elmore Leonard, the writer of the short story that *3:10 to Yuma* is based on, also wrote the novel *Rum Punch*, which was adapted by Quentin Tarantino for his film *Jackie Brown*. The Overland Stage Line was also seen in the John Ford film *Stagecoach*.

NOT YOUR MOTHER'S MILK

"It's Mother's Milk."
- The Dag from Mad Max: Fury Road

What must we drink, we who wander this Wasteland in search of our better selves? This, my friends, is not your mother's milk! You simply mix bourbon, simple syrup, pure vanilla extract, and whole milk. Then you drink! And then you mix again while riding valiantly into Valhalla! This sweet nectar is so shiny and chrome, it will take hold of you, and you will resent its absence.

Serves: 1

Ingredients:

1 1/2 oz Maker's Mark
  bourbon
1 1/2 oz simple syrup
3 oz whole milk
Dash of pure vanilla extract

Directions:

In a cocktail shaker with ice, add bourbon, simple syrup, milk, and vanilla.

Cover and shake vigorously until chilled. Strain into an old-fashioned milk bottle.

MAD MAX'S MEAT PIE

*"I am the one who runs from both
the living and the dead. Hunted by scavengers.
Haunted by those I could not protect. So I exist in this
wasteland. A man reduced to a single instinct: Survive."
- Max Rockatansky from Mad Max: Fury Road*

Tired of just surviving instead of thriving? Try this pie! It's a meat pie! And it's perfect! Perfect in every way! We scavenged The Wasteland high and low for the most furiously delicious ingredients, and branded the pie with Immortan Joe's logo. Served with greens freshly picked from the gardens of the Citadel, this meal is anything but mediocre. If you're gonna dine, you're gonna dine historic on the Fury Road!

MAD MAX'S MEAT PIE

Hands-On: 1 hr
To Plate: 1 hr 20 min
Serves: 4

Ingredients:

Mad Max's Meat Pie:
2 tbsp olive oil
1 medium yellow onion, finely chopped
1 cup celery, diced
1 cup carrots, diced
2 sprigs fresh thyme
1 lb sirloin steak, cubed, or two-headed lizard meat
5 slices prosciutto, chopped, or sliced desert beetle
Salt, to taste
Pepper, to taste
2 tbsp tomato paste
1 tbsp allspice
1/2 cup red wine
2 tbsp bourbon
1/2 cup milk
2 tbsp flour
2 packages pie dough
1 egg, white only

Citadel Greens:
2 cups spring mix salad greens
1/4 cup fresh mixed micro greens
1/4 cup fresh basil leaves, finely chopped
1/4 cup fresh chives, finely chopped
2 tsp fresh thyme, finely chopped

Red Wine Vinaigrette:
1/4 cup red wine vinegar
3/4 cup olive oil
1/4 tsp salt
1/4 tsp sugar
1/4 tsp black pepper
1/2 tsp Dijon mustard

Directions:

Mad Max's Meat Pie:
In a large heavy pot over medium-high heat, add olive oil, onion, celery, carrots, and thyme, then sauté until the vegetables are tender but not browned, about 5 minutes. Add the steak and prosciutto to the pot and season with salt and pepper. Cook, stirring often, until the meat is nicely browned, about 8 minutes. Add the tomato paste and allspice, then cook until the tomato paste is well blended. Stir in the wine and bourbon, and cook until most of it evaporates, about 4 minutes. Reduce the heat to medium, add the milk, and cook until the sauce is thick and creamy, about 4 minutes. Sprinkle the flour over the mixture and cook until well blended, about 1 minute.

Preheat oven to 375 degrees.

Roll out the pieces of pie dough to a 1/4-inch thickness and cut out four 7-inch disks.

Ball up the remaining dough and, on a lightly floured surface, roll out the dough to a 1/4-inch thickness and cut out four 6-inch disks for the covers.

Place the 7-inch disks at the bottom of each of the four 5-inch baking ramekins, letting the excess fall over the sides. Add the filling to each pie and brush the edges with egg wash. Top each pie with the 6-inch disks and, using a fork, crimp the edges of pie crust together. Cut off the excess.

Roll out the remaining pie dough to a 1/4-inch thickness. Using a cookie cutter, cut out four dough skull crests and place one on top of each pie.

Bake until the tops are golden brown, about 20 minutes.

Serve with Citadel greens and a nice cold glass of water.

Citadel Greens:
In a bowl, add all greens and gently toss to combine. Serve with red wine vinaigrette.

Red Wine Vinaigrette:
In a glass jar with a screw-on lid, combine all ingredients. Tighten lid and shake vigorously for 1 minute before serving.

In *Mad Max: Fury Road*, the War Boys are Immortan Joe's soldiers. They worship him, believing him to be a living god. Joe calls them "half-life" because they, along with most of the population, appear to have radiation-induced cancer and will not live long. The War Boys use healthy people, like Max, the "full-life" blood bag, for blood transfusions to extend their lives. They scar their bodies with images of car parts and worship V8 engines, believing them to be a source of power and a means to a glorious death.

SPACE SPUDS

"All natural, organic, Martian-grown potatoes.
You don't hear that every day, do you?"
- Mark Watney from The Martian

While Mark Watney's Martian potato, breakfast sausage, and ketchup combination may be out of this world, we decided to elevate it with our own recipe. A collection of roasted potatoes, mashed potatoes made with smoked cheddar, and purple skillet potatoes are served with Italian sausage and spicy homemade ketchup. While preparing this recipe, be sure to save a potato or two in case you need to start your own spud garden!

SPACE SPUDS

Hands-On: 45 min
To Plate: 1 hr 30 min
Serves: 4

Ingredients:

Space Sausage:
1 tbsp extra-virgin olive oil
4 spicy Italian sausages

Baked Potatoes:
1 cup small fingerling potatoes
2 tbsp olive oil
Maldon sea salt, to taste
Freshly ground black pepper, to taste

Purple Skillet Potatoes:
4 small purple potatoes
2 tbsp unsalted butter
1 tbsp red wine vinegar
1 shallot, thinly sliced
1 clove garlic, finely minced
1 sprig fresh rosemary
1 sprig fresh thyme
Pinch of crushed red pepper flakes
Sea salt, to taste
Freshly ground black pepper, to taste

Smoked Cheddar Mashed Potatoes:
3 large russet potatoes, peeled and quartered
4 tbsp unsalted butter, cold and cut into squares
1/2 cup heavy cream
14 oz smoked cheddar cheese, finely sliced
2 cloves garlic, finely minced
Kosher salt, to taste
Freshly ground black pepper, to taste

Hab Ketchup:
1 tbsp olive oil
1 small onion, finely chopped
2 cloves garlic, finely minced
1 tbsp tomato paste
1/2 tsp salt
1/2 tsp ground mustard
1/4 tsp smoked paprika
1/4 tsp ground allspice
1/2 tsp crushed red pepper flakes
1/4 tsp ground cloves
1/2 tsp cayenne pepper
1/4 cup brown sugar
2 tbsp apple cider vinegar
2 (8 oz) cans tomato sauce
Salt, to taste
Freshly ground black pepper, to taste

Directions:

Space Sausage:
In a large skillet over medium-high heat, heat the oil and cook the sausages until the internal temperature reaches 160 degrees.

Baked Potatoes:
Preheat oven to 400 degrees.

Line a baking sheet with foil. Rub potatoes with olive oil, and season with salt and pepper. Place potatoes onto prepared baking sheet and bake until fork tender, about 25 minutes.

Purple Skillet Potatoes:
Cut the potatoes into 1/4-inch slices.

In a bowl of cold water, add potato slices and let soak for 30 minutes. Drain and pat the slices dry with a paper towel.

In a skillet over medium heat, add butter. When the butter is melted, add the potato slices and spread them evenly on the bottom of the skillet. Add the vinegar, shallots, garlic, rosemary, thyme, and red pepper flakes. Then add salt and pepper, to taste. Cook until browned, about 3 to 5 minutes per side.

Smoked Cheddar Mashed Potatoes:
In a large pot with salted water, place the potatoes and bring to a boil. Reduce heat to medium-low and simmer until fork tender, about 30 minutes. Drain, transfer to a large bowl, and mash the potatoes.

In a large pot over low heat, add the mashed potatoes and butter, then stir. Gradually add the cream while stirring constantly. Add the cheese, garlic, salt, and pepper. Stir constantly until all the cheese has melted.

Hab Ketchup:
In a medium saucepan over medium heat, heat the oil. Sauté the onions until they begin to brown, about 6 minutes. Add the garlic and cook for 1 minute. Stir in the tomato paste, salt, mustard, paprika, allspice, cloves, and cayenne until fully combined. Stir in the brown sugar, vinegar, and tomato sauce. Reduce heat to a simmer and cook until thick, about 15 minutes. Add the mixture to a blender and blend until smooth. Season with salt and pepper, to taste.

It is possible to grow potatoes on Mars, though they would be dangerous to consume without taking the proper precautions. First, Mark would have to soak the Martian soil in water in order to rinse out the perchlorates, salts hazardous to humans. Second, since Mark uses human waste as fertilizer, he would have to use Mars' radiation to kill the pathogens in any waste that wasn't his. By using the nitrates in his crew's desiccated feces, along with the bacteria from his own, Mark would end up with a soil rich enough to grow his humble crop.

MARK'S MASHED POTATO TRUFFLES

"I'm gonna dip this potato in some crushed Vicodin.
And there's nobody who can stop me."
– Mark Watney from The Martian

Hey, there. Ran out of ketchup and not sure what else to do with your potatoes? Mash them up and make them into these sweet, chocolatey potato truffles. Yep, you read that right. Potato truffles. Instead of "crushed Vicodin", these little potato confections are dipped in powdered fruits, cocoa powder, and ground pistachios. Your taste buds will be over the moon (ahem, we meant Mars...) while enjoying these delicious sweets!

MARK'S MASHED POTATO TRUFFLES

Hands-On: 1 hr 5 min
To Plate: 4 hrs 25 min
Serves: 4

Ingredients:

2 large russet potatoes, peeled and quartered
4 tbsp butter, cut into squares
1/2 cup milk
2 tbsp heavy cream
Pinch of fine sea salt
2 cups dark chocolate chips
1 tsp pure vanilla extract
1/4 cup shelled unsalted pistachios, for topping
1/4 cup freeze-dried mango, for topping
1/4 cup freeze-dried raspberries, for topping
1/3 cup unsweetened cocoa powder, for topping
Cacao nibs, for garnish
Fresh mint sprigs, for garnish

Directions:

In a large pot with salted water, add the potatoes and bring to a boil. Reduce heat to medium-low and simmer until fork tender, about 20 minutes. Drain and transfer to the bowl of a stand mixer.

In a small saucepan over low heat, heat the butter, milk, and heavy cream until butter is nearly melted.

In the bowl of a stand mixer, add the milk mixture and sea salt. Blend until the potatoes are smooth and creamy. Let cool and place into the refrigerator to chill for 2 hours.

In a large microwave safe bowl, heat the dark chocolate chips at 50% power for 30 seconds, stir, and repeat until melted.

Combine the melted chocolate and pure vanilla extract with the mashed potatoes. Chill the mixture in the refrigerator for 30 minutes.

In a food processor, grind the pistachios to a fine powder, and place the powder in a small bowl.

Using a pestle and mortar, grind the freeze-dried mango to a powder, and place the powder in a small bowl.

Using a pestle and mortar, grind the freeze dried raspberries to a powder, and place the powder in another small bowl.

In a separate small bowl, add the cocoa powder.

Line a baking sheet with parchment paper.

Remove chocolate mixture from the refrigerator. Take 1 tablespoon-sized scoop of the chocolate-potato mixture and use your hands to form balls. Immediately roll the truffles into the toppings, alternating between the mango powder, raspberry powder, pistachio powder, and cocoa powder. Place each coated truffle onto the parchment-lined baking sheet and refrigerate until firm, about 30 minutes.

Before serving, garnish each plate with rows of cacao nibs and some fresh mint.

NASA Announced on September 28, 2015, just four days before *The Martian* premiered in the United States, that briny water had been discovered on the surface of Mars. The Mars Reconnaissance Orbiter (MRO), using an imaging spectrometer, detected hydrated minerals on slopes where the temperatures are above -10 degrees Fahrenheit. John Grunsfeld, associate administrator of NASA's Science Mission Directorate and former astronaut, stated, "This is a significant development, as it appears to confirm that water -- albeit briny -- is flowing today on the surface of Mars."

TURANDOT DUMPLINGS

"You want drama? Go to the opera."
– Ethan Hunt from Mission: Impossible - Rogue Nation

Turandot is a three-act opera about a beautiful Chinese princess. Whoever wishes to marry the princess must first answer three riddles. This perplexing dish is inspired by the suitor's dilemma. Three delicious duck dumplings each presented with a different sauce. Will you be able to identify each one? In the opera, an incorrect answer results in death, but here it results in more dumplings! Bravo!

TURANDOT DUMPLINGS

Hands-On: 1 hr
To Plate: 1 hr
Serves: 4

Ingredients:

Duck and Shiitake Fried Dumplings:
1 scallion, thinly sliced
3/4 tbsp fresh ginger, minced
1/2 tbsp soy sauce
1/2 tsp cornstarch
4 shiitake mushrooms, finely chopped
1/4 tsp sugar
4 oz spinach
1 duck breast, roasted
Round wonton wraps
Vegetable oil, for cooking

Curry Coconut Sauce:
6 tbsp coconut milk
1 tbsp red curry paste
3 tsp fresh lime juice
2 tsp soy sauce
2 tsp fish sauce
2 tsp honey
1 tsp fresh ginger, grated

Cilantro Garlic Sauce:
8 tsp garlic, minced
2 tbsp cilantro, finely chopped
4 tbsp fish sauce
4 tbsp fresh lime juice
1 tbsp light brown sugar
1 tsp red pepper flakes

Kimchi Butter Sauce:
6 tbsp unsalted butter
9 tbsp kimchi paste
1 tbsp honey
1 tsp sesame seeds, toasted

Directions:

Duck and Shiitake Fried Dumplings:
In a large bowl, add in the scallions, ginger, soy sauce, cornstarch, and mushrooms.

In a skillet, add a tablespoon of water, sugar, and spinach. Cook until wilted, about 30 seconds. When cool, drain excess liquid and finely chop the spinach. Add spinach to the bowl with the mushrooms.

Finely shred the roasted duck and add it to the bowl with the mushrooms. Combine all the ingredients together.

Place 1 tablespoon of filling into each wrap and seal the dumpling.

In a skillet over high heat, heat 2 tablespoons of vegetable oil until shimmering. Cook the dumplings for 1 minute, then add 1/2 cup of water , or enough to come 1/3 of the way up the side of the dumplings. Cover pan, bring to a boil, and allow the water to be absorbed, about 3 minutes. Remove lid, reduce heat to medium, and cook 3 more minutes. The water should be completely evaporated.

Serve dumplings with the three sauces.

Curry Coconut Sauce:
In a small saucepan over medium heat, bring milk and curry paste to a simmer. Cook for 30 seconds, then remove from heat.

In a small bowl, combine lime juice, soy sauce, fish sauce, honey, and ginger. Add curry milk mixture and combine.

Cilantro Garlic Sauce:
In a small bowl, combine the garlic, cilantro, fish sauce, lime juice, sugar, and chili flakes.

Kimchi Butter Sauce:
In a small saucepan over low heat, melt butter. Add kimchi paste, honey, sesame seeds, and continue to cook until well combined, whisking constantly to create a sauce.

Mission: Impossible – Rogue Nation's filmmakers decided on the color of Ilsa's dress through a process of elimination. Paula Patton wore a green dress in *Mission: Impossible - Ghost Protocol*, Maggie Q wore a red dress in *Mission: Impossible III*, and they did not want go with either black or white. This resulted in a bright yellow dress being chosen for Ilsa to wear, which might not exactly be the best color for someone trying to hide in the shadows.

MOROCCAN CHEESECAKE

"And what brings you gentlemen to Casablanca?"
- Ilsa Faust from Mission: Impossible - Rogue Nation

Made with goat's cheese, cream cheese, and condensed milk, this Moroccan-style cheesecake remains creamy inside while the lightly toasted almonds create the crunch needed to keep your sweet tooth engaged. The cheesecake is garnished with fresh berries and pairs well with a honey-lemon and sun-dried tomato vinaigrette. The mission for dessert doesn't have to be impossible.

MOROCCAN CHEESECAKE

Hands-On: 35 min
To Plate: 1 hr 30 min
Serves: 4

Ingredients:

Moroccan Cheesecakes:
2 1/2 cups cornflakes
6 tbsp almonds, toasted
16 tbsp unsalted butter, melted
2 tbsp honey
14 oz sweetened condensed milk
Juice of 2 lemons
Zest of 1 lemon
1 cup cream cheese
1/2 cup chèvre
3 eggs
2 figs
1 cup blackberries
Mint leaves

Honey-Lemon Vinaigrette:
2 tbsp honey
3 tbsp lemon juice
3 tbsp extra-virgin olive oil
Sun-dried tomatoes, finely
  chopped
Salt and pepper, to taste

Directions:

Moroccan Cheesecakes:
Preheat oven to 350 degrees.

In a food processor, add the cornflakes and almonds, then chop into fine crumbs. Next add the butter and honey, then mix to create a crumble.

Grease mini muffin pans with cooking spray, and add the almond crumble to the bottom of each cup.

In a large bowl, add the condensed milk, lemon juice, and zest, then combine. Add the cream cheese and chèvre, then mix well until fully incorporated.

Separate the egg yolks from the egg whites. Incorporate the yolks into the cheese mixture.

In a bowl, whisk the egg whites until stiff peaks form. Slowly fold the egg whites into the cheese mixture. Spoon the mixture into the mini muffin pans. Bake for 15 minutes, allow to cool, then chill in the refrigerator for 30 minutes.

Stack the mini-cheesecakes on top of one another, garnish with half a fig and some blackberries, and serve with the honey-lemon vinaigrette.

Honey-Lemon Vinaigrette:
In a bowl, whisk together the honey, lemon juice, olive oil, tomatoes, salt, and pepper.

Rebecca Ferguson used Hollywood screen legend and fellow Swedish actress Ingrid Bergman as inspiration to play her character in *Mission: Impossible – Rogue Nation*. The name Ilsa Faust and the film's setting in the city of Casablanca are clear references to Bergman's character Ilsa Lund in the 1942 cinematic classic *Casablanca*.

REVENGE

"My heart bleeds...
But revenge is in the creator's hands."
- Hikuc from The Revenant

This dish is 'Revenge', which, as we all know, is best served cold. The icy dessert incorporates various berries native to the American West; fresh blackberries, fresh raspberries, chokecherry jelly, and huckleberry syrup are blended and frozen into a flaky granita. Topped with tangy whipped crème fraîche and a deliciously symbolic white chocolate spiral, this bittersweet treat is worth the wait.

REVENGE

Hands-On: 1 hr 10 min
To Plate: 4 hrs 15 min
Serves: 4

Ingredients:

Granita:
2 cups blackberries, plus more
  for garnish
1 cup raspberries, plus more for
  garnish
1 cup chokecherry jelly
1/4 cup huckleberry syrup
2 tbsp crème de cassis
1 tbsp fresh lemon juice
3/4 cup water

Whipped Crème Fraîche:
3/4 cups chilled whipping cream
1/4 cup chilled sour cream
1/4 cup powdered sugar
1/4 tsp pure vanilla extract

Spiral:
1 cup white chocolate chips

Directions:

Granita:
In a blender, add the blackberries, raspberries, jelly, syrup, crème de cassis, lemon juice, and water. Purée until smooth. Strain through a fine-mesh sieve into a large baking pan.

Freeze mixture until edges begin to set, about 30 minutes. Using a fork, scrape up the frozen portions. Freeze for 30 minutes then scrape. Repeat this process every 30 minutes until mixture resembles fluffy shaved ice, for about 4 hours.

Serve granita with fresh berries, a dollop of whipped crème fraîche and a chocolate spiral.

Whipped Crème Fraîche:
In the bowl of an electric mixer, add whipping cream, sour cream, sugar, and vanilla, then beat until stiff peaks form.

Spiral:
In a microwave safe bowl, heat the chocolate at 50% power for 30 seconds, stir, and repeat until melted. Quickly place melted chocolate into a piping bag.

Lay parchment paper on a baking tray. Using the piping bag, create 4 spirals. Place baking tray in freezer and allow to harden, about 15 minutes.

The Revenant's vicious grizzly bear attack was filmed with two stuntmen wearing blue body suits and foam bear head helmets so that Leonardo DiCaprio would have a target to hit while fighting back. Leo also wore a stunt harness that assisted the stuntmen in whipping him around. The attack consists of 21 total shots, 16 of which were pieced together into one seamless six-minute sequence. New prosthetics were applied to Leo between takes to show the progression of his wounds. In post-production, the stuntmen were replaced with a CG bear crafted by ILM.

POLPO DI SPECTRE

*"If you go there, you're crossing over to
a place where there is no mercy."*
- Lucia Sciarra from SPECTRE

Welcome, reader. It's been a long time. And, finally, here we are. What took you so long? The mission is simple: we're giving you the license to grill this armed and delicious octopus. It must be devoured immediately! The flavorful tentacles are grilled and served with spicy chorizo sausage and accompanied by a smoky red pepper sauce. We don't expect you to talk. We expect you to dine!

POLPO DI SPECTRE

Hands-On: 35 min
To Plate: 1 hr 35 min
Serves: 4

Ingredients:

Octopus:
1 bottle dry white wine
1 wine cork
2 cups water
2 sprigs fresh Italian parsley
2 bay leaves
2 tbsp red pepper flakes
2 tbsp whole coriander seeds
2 tbsp whole peppercorns
2 cloves garlic, peeled and
    halved
1 small onion, peeled and
    quartered
1 lemon, halved
Fine sea salt, to taste
Freshly ground black pepper, to
    taste
12 octopus tentacles
1/4 cup olive oil
1 fresh red chili pepper, sliced

Chorizo:
2 tsp olive oil
2 chorizo casero

Roasted Red Pepper Purée:
1 (12 oz) jar fire roasted red
    peppers
2 garlic cloves
1 tbsp extra-virgin olive oil
1 tbsp balsamic vinegar
1/2 tsp crushed red pepper
1/2 tsp cayenne pepper
1/2 tsp paprika
1 tbsp sugar
Fine sea salt, to taste
Freshly ground black pepper, to
    taste

Directions:

Octopus:
In a large pot, add the wine, cork, water, parsley, bay leaves, red pepper flakes, coriander seeds, peppercorns, garlic, onion, lemon, salt, and pepper. Bring to a boil. Add the octopus, reduce heat to a simmer, and cook tentacles until they are tender enough to be pierced with a sharp knife. Check for tenderness at 45 minutes, but it could take up to 90 minutes. Remove tentacles from the pot and allow them to drain.

Preheat grill to high heat.

In a bowl, toss the tentacles in olive oil and season with salt and pepper. Grill the tentacles until well browned, about 3 to 4 minutes per side.

Serve with roasted red pepper purée, chorizo, and garnish with balsamic vinegar and several slices of red chili pepper.

Chorizo:
In a sauté pan over medium heat, add olive oil and chorizo slices. Cook for about 3 minutes per side.

Roasted Red Pepper Purée:
In a food processor, add the peppers, garlic, oil, vinegar, crushed red pepper, cayenne pepper, paprika, sugar, salt, and freshly ground black pepper. Purée the mixture until smooth and strain.

The cracks in the glass caused by Bond shooting at Blofeld look very similar to the SPECTRE octopus insignia. This same octopus-like pattern in cracked glass was used in the film's promotional materials, including trailers and posters.

THE CUCKOO NEST

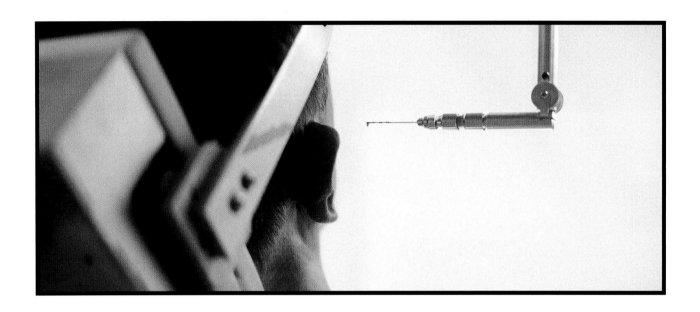

"Well, this cuckoo made me realize my father's life had to end.
In a way, he's responsible for the path I took.
So, thank you, cuckoo!"
– Franz Oberhauser from SPECTRE

There's only one bird call you need to know to enjoy this elegant dessert: "Cuckoo!" Created with sweet, crunchy fried dough, decadent chocolate cake, and chocolate "twigs", this is truly a nest you'll want to steal. The eggs, made with crumbled white cake and frosting, are brooding with sweetness. The things that bring people together. Out of simple ingredients, beauty.

THE CUCKOO NEST

Hands-On: 1 hr 35 min
To Plate: 5 hrs 20 min
Serves: 4

Ingredients:

The Nest:

2 cups powdered sugar
1 1/4 cups all-purpose flour
1/2 tsp ground cinnamon
1/8 tsp salt
6 large egg whites, lightly beaten
1 tsp pure vanilla extract
10 1/2 tbsp unsalted butter,
    melted and cooled to room
    temperature
1 tbsp heavy cream
Oil for frying

The Eggs:

1 box Pillsbury Moist Supreme
    Classic White Cake Mix
1/3 cup oil
3 eggs
Cooking spray
1 cup Pillsbury Creamy
    Supreme Classic White
    Frosting

Chocolate Cake:

1 box Pillsbury Moist Supreme
    Chocolate Cake Mix
1/3 cup oil
3 eggs
Cooking spray

Chocolate Twigs:

1/2 cup semisweet chocolate
    chips

Assembly/Garnish:

Micro flowers
Fresh blueberries
Fresh raspberries

Directions:

The Nest:

In a large bowl, sift together the powdered sugar, flour, cinnamon, and salt. Mix until well combined. Make a well in the center of the dry ingredients, and then add the eggs, vanilla, melted butter, and heavy cream. Gently whisk the ingredients together until well combined and the batter is creamy and smooth. Strain the batter through a fine mesh sieve into a clean bowl. Cover the bowl with plastic wrap and refrigerate for 4 hours.

In a deep fryer, heat oil to 375 degrees.

Pour the chilled batter into a piping bag fitted with a round tip. Carefully squeeze out the batter into the hot oil, creating a loop of batter inside the pan. When the dough is golden brown, remove it from the oil and allow to dry on paper towels.

The Eggs:

Preheat oven to 350 degrees.

In a large bowl, add cake mix, oil, and eggs. Mix until well combined.

Grease a 13 x 9-inch cake pan, pour in the mixture, and then bake until a toothpick inserted into the cake comes out clean, about 35 minutes. Allow the cake to cool completely before removing it from the pan. Crumble three cups of the cake and place it in a bowl. Add the frosting and mix well. Place the mixture in the freezer until it reaches the consistency of soft clay, about 2 hours.

When the mixture is firm enough, use your hands to form it into eggs.

Chocolate Cake:

Preheat oven 350 degrees.

In a large bowl, add cake mix, oil, and eggs. Mix until well combined.

Grease a 13 x 9-inch cake pan, pour in the mixture, and then bake until a toothpick inserted into the cake comes out clean, about 35 minutes. Allow the cake to cool completely before removing it from the pan.

Using a 3-inch round biscuit cutter, cut out 4 pieces of cake, place onto serving plates, and set aside. These will be the base of the "nests". Reserve the rest of the cake.

Chocolate Twigs:

Line a baking tray with parchment paper.

In a microwave safe bowl, heat the semi-sweet chocolate chips at 50% power for 30 seconds, stir, and repeat until melted. Using a spoon, drizzle several streaks of chocolate onto the parchment paper. Chill the chocolate in the freezer and allow it to harden, about 30 minutes.

Assembly/Garnish:

Using the fried batter, create a nest around each 3-inch chocolate cake. Place 2 eggs in the center of each nest and crumble the remaining chocolate cake around the nest. Garnish with chocolate twigs, flowers, blueberries, and raspberries.

Some have likened the torture scene in *SPECTRE* to the iconic laser scene in 1964's *Goldfinger*. However, the torture scene in *SPECTRE* hints more to the events of the first James Bond continuation novel, 1968's *Colonel Sun*. The novel has a chapter titled "The Theory And Practice Of Torture" in which Bond is strapped to a chair and has his head probed with tiny skewers. The titular Colonel Sun also explains to Bond how a man lives inside his head, and recalls once witnessing a man losing his eyes and being "gone" afterwards.

GENERAL HUX'S CHICKEN

"All remaining systems will bow to the First Order
and will remember this as the last day of the Republic!"
- General Hux from Star Wars: The Force Awakens

Bring all those who would rebel against you to their knees with this fiery chicken dish. A reinterpretation of the classic General Tso's chicken, this meal also marries sweetness and spice but adds hints of pineapple and the gentle tartness of the ponzu sauce. While the rogues of the Resistance plot against the First Order, you will plunge your fork deep into this aromatic Asian dish.

GENERAL HUX'S CHICKEN

Hands-On: 30 min
To Plate: 55 min
Serves: 4

Ingredients:

General Hux's Chicken:

4 tbsp cornstarch
2 egg yolks
1 tbsp soy sauce
1 lb chicken breast, cubed
Peanut oil, for frying
4 red chili peppers, sliced into strips
1 tbsp ginger, minced
4 garlic cloves, thinly sliced
2 tsp sesame oil
Brown rice, cooked
3 green onions, chopped

First Order Sauce:

1 cup chicken stock
2 tbsp soy sauce
2 tbsp brown sugar
2 tbsp malt vinegar
4 tbsp tomato paste
2 tsp corn starch
1 tbsp roasted red chili paste
2 tbsp ponzu sauce
2 tbsp pineapple preserves
2 tbsp Korean red pepper flakes, plus more for garnish

Directions:

In a bowl, whisk together the cornstarch, egg yolks, and the soy sauce. Add the chicken, making sure each piece is completely coated with the mixture. Allow the chicken to marinate at room temperature for 30 minutes.

In a large bowl, whisk together all of the ingredients for the First Order Sauce. Set aside.

In a large skillet, add just enough peanut oil to be able to submerge the chicken pieces. Heat oil to 350 degrees. Working in batches, begin frying the marinated chicken chunks. Fry the chicken until golden brown on all sides, about 3 minutes.

In a large sauté pan over high heat, heat 3 tablespoons of peanut oil. Add the sliced chili peppers and cook until almost blackened, about 1 minute. Add the ginger, garlic, and sesame oil, then cook until fragrant, about 30 seconds. Add the fried chicken pieces and The First Order Sauce, and then cook until the sauce has thickened slightly, about 3 minutes.

Serve with brown rice and garnish with green onions and Korean red pepper flakes.

Starkiller Base shares the same name as Luke Skywalker's original surname in an early draft of the script for 1977's *Star Wars: Episode IV – A New Hope*. The name "Starkiller" was also used as a codename for the main character in the 2008 video game *Star Wars: The Force Unleashed*.

JAKKU MUFFINS

"What you brought me today is
worth, hmmmm, one quarter portion."
- Unkar Plutt from Star Wars: The Force Awakens

When the stingy Unkar Plutt only grants you a quarter portion, make the best of it by creating this simple and healthy Jakku muffin. The matcha powder, finely ground tea leaves, adds a delicious earthy flavor that matches perfectly with the pistachios and lemon zest. The flaxseed, one of the oldest fiber crops in the world, contribute both fiber and micronutrients to the tasty muffin. Eaten by themselves or in combination with the tart Cape gooseberries, the Jakku muffins are the ideal dessert for any young Jedi.

JAKKU MUFFINS

Hands-On: 15 min
To Plate: 40 min
Serves: 4

Ingredients:

2 tbsp flaxseed
3/4 cup milk
1 1/2 cups pastry flour
2 tsp baking powder
1 tbsp matcha powder
1/2 cup pistachios, ground
1 tbsp lemon zest
1 tsp cinnamon
1/2 tsp nutmeg
1/8 tsp salt
1/2 cup margarine, melted
1/2 cup brown sugar
2 tsp vanilla extract
1/4 cup pistachios, chopped
Honey, for garnish
12 fresh Cape gooseberries

Directions:

In a small bowl, combine the flaxseed and milk. Let the flaxseed marinate in the milk until softened, about 15 minutes.

Preheat oven to 375 degrees.

In a bowl, combine flour, baking powder, matcha, ground pistachios, zest, cinnamon, nutmeg, and salt.

In the bowl of an electric mixer, add the margarine, sugar, and vanilla, and then blend until creamy. Add the milk and flaxseed mixture, and continue blending until fully incorporated. Add the flour mixture, a third at a time, and continue blending until fully incorporated.

In half-circle silicone molds, add the muffin batter and bake until a toothpick inserted into each muffin comes out clean, about 15 minutes. Allow the muffins to reach room temperature before removing from the molds.

Top each muffin with honey and chopped pistachios. Garnish with fresh Cape gooseberries.

The instant bread that Rey makes for herself, called polystarch on Jakku, was not created using CGI. The special effects artists used vacuums to suck the water out of the bowl and simultaneously make the bread "rise". It took the crew three months to figure out how to pull off the effect and, by all accounts, the bread tasted terrible.

POOLJOB
CHIMICHANGA

"I'd love a blow job. The drink, moose knuckle!"
- Wade Wilson from Deadpool

Oh, hello! Fancy a blow job? You know, the drink. Just pour some Kahlúa and Baileys into a shot glass and top with whipped cream. Then, place your hands behind your back, carefully pick up the shot glass with your mouth, tilt your head back, and don't forget to swallow. After that, it's time to make the chimi-effin-changas! Even if you don't like chimichangas all that much, you'll still love to say it. Try it out. Chimichanga. Chimichanga. Chimichanga.

Serves: 1

Ingredients:

Blow Job:
1 oz Kahlúa
1/2 oz Baileys Irish Cream
Whipped cream, for topping

Deadpool Chimichangas:
2 tbsp grapeseed oil
1 small yellow onion, diced
2 garlic cloves, minced
1 jalapeño, seeded and
　minced
1/2 lb Mexican chorizo
Salt, to taste
Black pepper, to taste
4 mini flour tortillas
Peanut oil, for frying
1/2 cup sharp cheddar
　cheese, shredded
1/2 cup Mexican salsa
2 tbsp fresh cilantro, minced

Directions:

Blow Job:
Pour Kahlúa and Baileys into a shot glass and top it with whipped cream.

Deadpool Chimichangas:
In a skillet over medium-high heat, add oil and onions. Cook until softened, about 5 minutes. Reduce heat to medium, add garlic, and continue cooking the garlic until it begins to brown. Raise heat to medium-high, add jalapeño and chorizo, then cook until the chorizo is cooked through. Season with salt and pepper. Place cooked chorizo in a strainer to remove any excess oil, and to allow the meat to cool before placing in tortillas.

In a skillet over medium heat, carefully warm the tortillas until warmed through and pliable.

In a saucepan, warm peanut oil to 350 degrees.

Place about 2 tablespoons of chorizo into each tortilla. Fold the sides of the tortilla towards the center, like a burrito, and use toothpicks to hold the folds in place. One at a time, carefully fry the stuffed tortillas until golden, about 1 minute.

Using a spider strainer, remove fried chimichangas from the oil. Top with cheese, salsa, and cilantro.

Index

Cocktails

Desserts

Desserts Cont.

Donuts: Lemon, Powdered Sugar, 182

Granita: Blackberry, Raspberry, Chokecherry Jelly, Huckleberry Syrup, 228

Muffins: Matcha, Flaxseed, Pistachio, 244

Pie: Mango, 170

Strudel: Apple, Cream, 148

Tart: Apple, Strawberry Glaze, 22

Tart: Coffee, Dark Chocolate, Blood Oranges, 202

Truffles: Chocolate, 116

Truffles: Chocolate, Potato, 216

Waffles: Banana-Apricot, Amaretto-Apricot Syrup, 190

Meat

Beef, Brisket: Beef Stock, Pearl Onions, Dry Rub, German Potato Salad, 144

Beef, Burger: Potato Latke, Kosher Gherkin, Apple Sauce, 128

Beef, Chuck: Red Wine, Bacon, Potatoes, Carrots, 46

Beef, Ribs: Bourbon-Cherry Barbeque Sauce, Cherry Salsa, Potato Wedges, 68

Beef, Sirloin Steak: Pie Dough, Prosciutto, Salad Greens, 208

Lamb, Chops: Adobo, 94

Lamb, Loin: Mint Sauce, 122

Meatballs: Beef, Pork, Veal, Italian Sausage, Tomato Sauce, Pasta, 54

Pork, Loin: Soy Sauce, Ginger, Bacon-Wrapped Dates, Peach Crostini, 186

Sausage, Chorizo: Chimichanga, Salsa, 246

Sausage, Italian: Potatoes, Spicy Ketchup, 212

Poultry

Chicken, Breast: Orange Juice, Red Chile, Cilantro, Quinoa, Black Beans, 132

Chicken, Breast: Ponzu Sauce, Brown Rice, 240

Chicken, Breast: Spinach, Italian Sausage, Red Wine Sauce, Cherries, Figs, 196

Chicken, Liver: Chianti Reduction, Fava Beans, 108

Chicken, Tenderloins: Chestnut Flour, Cheddar Cheese, Chives, 26

Duck, Breast: Dumplings, Curry Sauce, Cilantro Sauce, Kimchi Sauce, 220

Turkey Breast: Duck Breast, Chicken Breast, Italian Sausage, 158

Seafood

Clams, Manila: Heavy Cream, Idaho Potatoes, 64

Crab, Soft-Shell: Arepas, Grapefruit Salsa, Orange-Papaya Purée, 88

Lobster, Maine: Brandy, Caviar, Heavy Cream, 18

Mahi-Mahi: Garlic, Lime Juice, Lime Zest, Conch Salad, Mousseline Sauce, 166

Octopus: Red Pepper Sauce, Chorizo, 232

Scallops: Beets, Arugula, Oranges, 10

Shrimp: Scallops, Angel Hair Pasta, White Wine Sauce, 78

Shrimp: Lemon, Coconut, Lemon Sauce, Pineapple Sauce, 112

Behind the Scenes

Every day that we work on movies we find inspirations, and through these inspirations we discover new ingredients and techniques. As children, we're told not to play with our food, but now, bound only by the limits of our imaginations, we are free to explore, combine, mash together, and ultimately eat our creations. A lot of work goes into creating the final product, and the following pages are just a few examples of what we do "behind the scenes".

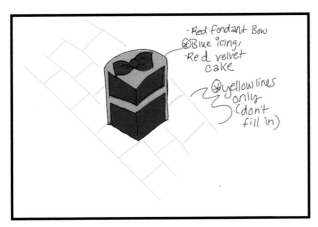  

Every recipe is born from an inspiration. By allowing ourselves to become inspired by the scenes we love, images begin to emerge. When Dorothy takes her first steps onto the Yellow Brick Road in her iconic Ruby Red Slippers, images of red velvet cakes over a tart lemon curd began to materialize. There was a bit of a learning curve involved in making the red fondant bows for "Dorothy's Ruby Red Cake", but after a few failed attempts, we were back on the Yellow Brick Road.

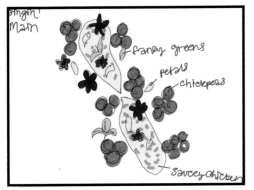  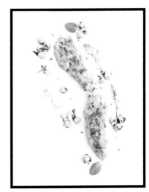

Don Lockwood and Cosmo Brown tormenting the diction coach in the "Moses Supposes" number is probably one of the most entertaining and humorous scenes in *Singin' in the Rain*, or any musical for that matter! Our inspiration came from the Diction Coach's use of the "Ch-" words, and our challenge was to create a charming chicken dish that would incorporate as many "Ch-" ingredients as possible but still taste amazing! Our small garden provided many wonderful herbs to choose from.

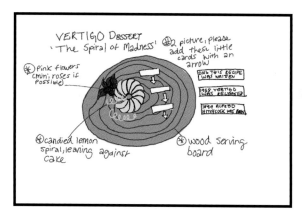  

As a master of suspense, Alfred Hitchcock uses imagery in *Vertigo* that is both cryptic and beautiful. For our "Spiral of Madness" dessert, we wanted to recreate the labeled cross-section of the giant redwood from the haunting scene in the Muir Woods. The spirals were a recurring theme in the film, and when we discovered this spiral shaped bundtlette pan, we knew we had the perfect mold. The best part was testing the recipe.

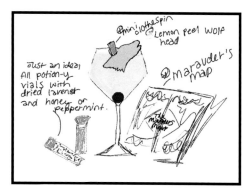  

Growing up with the *Harry Potter* movies was a magical experience. Needless to say, we are huge *Potter* fans and, as you can tell from our book, huge fans of fancy cocktails as well. It's hard to pick a favorite movie from the series, but if we had to pick, it would be *Prisoner of Azkaban*! In the movie, Professor Remus Lupin uses a potion to help relieve his lycanthropic symptoms, so we wanted to create a cocktail that made us feel like we were brewing a our own version of the potion, using lavender rather than wolfsbane. Creating the Marauder's Map was easy. Carving werewolf heads out of lemon peels, not so much.

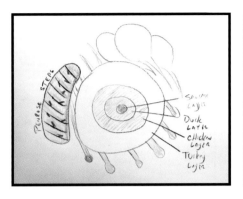  

After we find our inspiration within a movie, the recipe is sketched out before any food is prepared. Much like Ariadne drawing a maze for Cobb in *Inception*, it becomes the blueprint for our next quixotic adventure. While we try our best to stay true to the conceptual sketch, food has no master and will do as it pleases while it roasts, boils, and broils its way to the desired temperature.

Props help give personality to the photos and help the viewers identify the movie that inspired the recipe. Up until now, the props have been items we've either made or borrowed. For *Alice in Wonderland*, we knew we wanted to incorporate tea into the cocktail, and what better mascot for this drink than a white rabbit? This adorable white rabbit is named Spook. He seemed to have a good time sliding around the set on his little lucky paws and, lucky for us, he didn't destroy the fine china given to one of our team members by her great-grandmother.

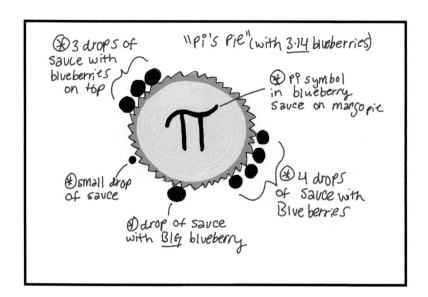

Sometimes, it's all about the tiny details. For "Pi's Pie", we knew that we somehow wanted to incorporate the Pi symbol and 3.14 into the photo. We decided to garnish the plate with "3.14" blueberries. We had to sift through dozens of blueberries to find just the right sizes for the picture!

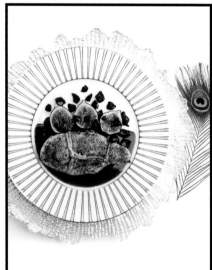

The best thing about creating recipes for *Fifty Shades of Grey* was doing the research. We got hardcore into learning the proper "bondage" techniques for these chicken breasts. It felt a little weird getting so kinky with food. Ultimately, the final photo gave us great pleasure, with very little pain.

Fin

Film and Fork
will return!